# Let's Explore The Shore

# LET'S EXPLORE
# THE SHORE

by ILKA LIST MAIDOFF
Illustrated by the Author

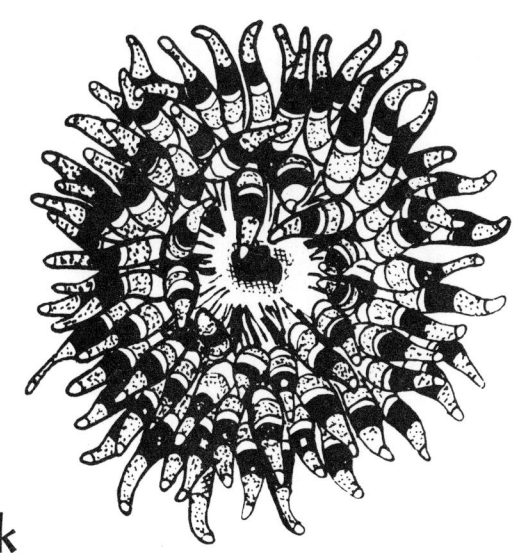

an Astor Book

IVAN OBOLENSKY, INC. •
New York

*Copyright © 1962 by Ivan Obolensky, Inc.*

*All Rights Reserved*

*Library of Congress Catalog Card Number: 62-18795*

*First Printing*

*Manufactured in the United States of America*

*This Book is for Jules, Lee and Jonah*

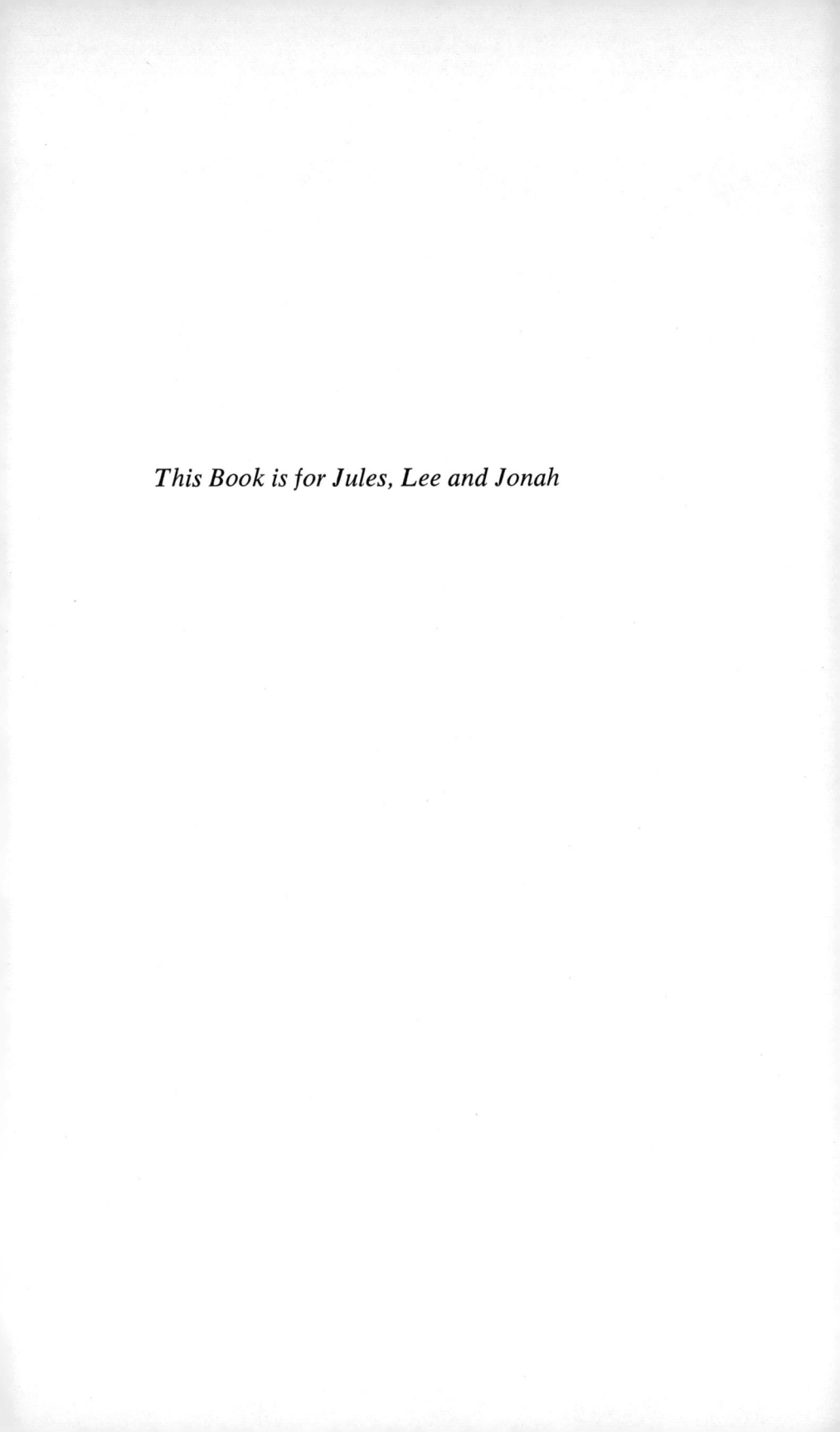

# ACKNOWLEDGEMENTS

*I am grateful and indebted to my former professor at St. Andrews University, Dr. James M. Dodd, now Head of the Department of Zoology of the University of Leeds, for checking my manuscript for accuracy, and kindly writing a preface; to my husband for his belief in me and his understanding of the problems involved in creating a book; and to my parents, Phyllis and Albert List, for their steadfast faith in my endeavors.*

# PREFACE

I have yet to meet anyone not fascinated by the living things of the seashore and any book which helps its readers to indulge this fascination to greater profit and pleasure has my warmest support. This is such a book, and I am particularly glad to write these words of introduction since its author learned at least some of her marine zoology with me when she was a visiting student in the University of St. Andrews in Scotland. I well remember from that time her artistic talents and in this volume these combine with a literary flair and a love of animals to produce a delightful book which will give you, its reader, the greatest possible pleasure and may even persuade some of you to take up marine zoology as a career. I hope so!

The study of marine life has always had a special attraction for zoologists, both professional and amateur, and no wonder! There is an anonymous verse* which runs:—

If all the sea
were one sea
That would be
1,370,232,000,000,000,000,000,000 cc.

This is a great deal of water (some 301,471,060,000,000,000,000 gallons to express it in more familiar terms) and it harbors a staggering variety and number of living things. Of course there is not one sea but several seas, and these cover some seven-tenths of the earth's surface and wash uncountable miles of shore. These shores vary in extent from a foot or so to many yards and one finds a profusion of living things, both plants and animals, unequalled elsewhere on the face of the earth. It is clear that conditions on different shores will vary a great deal, as will conditions in different parts of the same shore. Living things have been ruthlessly selected during evolutionary time by the rigors of their surroundings and nowhere is this better seen than in the animals and plants inhabiting the intertidal region. Study of the special features which enable living things to occupy particular situations

* Quoted by Dr. James Fraser in his recent book, *Nature Adrift*.

has a special fascination and I commend it to readers of this book who wish to put what they learn from it to practical use.

There is, as I have said, a wide range of physical conditions between high and low tide levels and few shore animals (limpets are almost an exception) are fitted to them all. They are therefore zoned, often strikingly, and the dominant animal or plant of a particular zone gives its name to that zone; thus we have the periwinkle zone, the barnacle zone, and so on. It is true that the seaweeds often demonstrate the zones better than do the animals, probably because, since they are attached, their range is more strictly circumscribed; and although this book is limited to the common shore animals, I am sure you will give at least superficial attention to their botanical neighbors when you are investigating for yourselves, in their natural surroundings, the animals that are so fascinatingly described in the following pages.

Every large group in the animal kingdom is represented in the intertidal fauna and to choose a representative series is a difficult task indeed, even for a book much larger than this one, but the author has succeeded in choosing examples representative of virtually all the large groups of animals without backbones, and those she writes about are large enough to be easily seen and studied, and are generally present in large numbers. Most of them offer opportunities for the study of the features which adapt them to a particular niche on the shore, and all of them are found throughout the world. It is a remarkable fact that had she written her book during her stay in St. Andrews, she might well have chosen the same species to illustrate life on those cold exposed North Sea shores as she has chosen here. On other shores, the Pacific Coast of North America, for example, the species are different but most of them are easily recognizable as larger cousins of the limpets, periwinkles, barnacles, etc., here described.

You will learn here a great deal about the construction of some of the common shore animals and about their daily lives, their relations with their neighbors, their struggle for existence, and the lengths of their lives. I feel sure the book will give pleasure to all who read it, of whatever age, and I echo the hope expressed by its author in her introduction that it will help you, its reader, to discover a world you may often have looked at, but never truly seen.

                        Professor James M. Dodd
                        Head
                        Department of Zoology
                        Leeds University
                        England

# INTRODUCTION

People of every age, in all of time, have been fascinated by water. I am no exception. I have always loved small brooks, rivers, ponds, and lakes (not to mention puddles, gutter streams, tubs, sinks, and potfuls as a child), but my special love is the sea. The sea, perhaps because it is infinitely large and immeasurably deep, provokes in me many unaccountable emotions. I like to be near it. I enjoy seeing it lie serene under the sun, and I am excited when I find it seething with contained rage and power on a gray, windy day. I enjoy the saltiness when I am swimming, even though it stings my eyes. I like to float in boats, and, together with sportsmen who do not really fish for food, I find pleasure pulling strange creatures up on hooks.

Perhaps somewhere within us there remains a sense of the origin of life in the sea eons ago. Surely our bodies, which are largely made of salty mineral water, remind us both of our connection with, and emancipation from, the sea. If these reflections seem too remote, we can turn our backs on the impersonal depths of the open ocean, and observe the shore, where the sea intimately reveals its profundity in the cracks and crevices, the tidal pools, under seaweeds, and on the bare washed rocks themselves.

At the shore, where the land meets the sea, there is a zone that has been held forever in the grip of the tides. There live hundreds of different animals and plants, in places which are muddy, sandy, or completely rocky. All of these places are twice daily covered with water, and twice daily exposed to sun, wind, rain, and air. Not only do living things here feel the effects of the weather, of which we humans constantly complain, but they are pounded by the waves, winter and summer.

Doesn't it seem impossible that real plants and small animals can survive the cold exposure of winter, the sunny glare in summer, and the fresh water rainfalls at low tide? But it is not impossible, for the plants and creatures living in this narrow strip are well adapted to their lives, and do not merely survive, but multiply.

Whenever and wherever you are by the sea, it is a simple matter to visit the tidal zone. There, only protective shoes and a sharp eye are necessary to reveal most, or all, of the animals I talk about in the chapters following. Patience and a few prods and pokes will show you a great deal about their habits. Quiet observation will allow you to discover the interrelationships of the animals, and repeated visits will reveal the beauties of the rocks and pools. I hope that this book will accompany you to the shore and help you to discover a world you may have often looked at, but never truly seen.

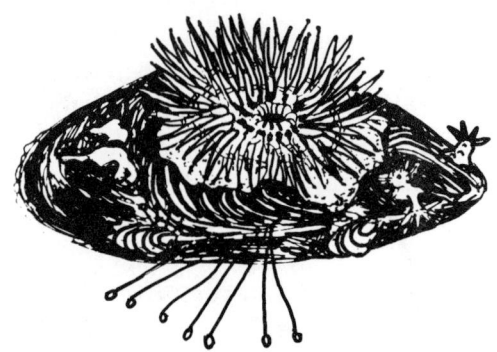

# CONTENTS

Preface · vii

Introduction · ix

1. Chalk Fortresses · 1
2. The Irresistible Radula · 12
3. Hanging by a Thread · 21
4. A Close and Deadly Embrace · 28
5. Sea Urchins · 37
6. Hunchbacks by the Hundreds · 46
7. The Lucky Instinct · 55
8. The Busy Strainer · 61
9. The Flower Animal · 67
10. Floating Umbrellas · 76
11. A Friendly Hermit · 83
12. The Cautious Crab · 89
13. Hide and Seek · 94
14. Lobsters, Red and Green · 100

# Let's Explore The Shore

# CHALK FORTRESSES

CHAPTER 1

Again and again the waves spill heavily over the rocks, along the shore. They pour into cracks and pools, crowd in between the strands of seaweed, and search for ways to return to the sea. Each time they break on the wet, lavender rocks, thousands of little barnacles open trap doors and kick their feet in welcome. When you see tiny barnacles perched on the side of a rock, facing the vast ocean, it is surprising to see them greet the waves so gladly, unafraid of the sucking undertow of retreating water. Neither you nor I would dream of sitting there absolutely quietly, letting the waves pound and drench us. We would consider it far too dangerous. Barnacles obviously do not.

A barnacle has no eyes and does not judge the waves by their size and style. Each barnacle is securely fastened to the rocks, and what matters to him is the amount of food the ocean water carries in it. A friendly sea to a barnacle is a sea full of microscopic food. A dangerous sea is not a rough sea but an empty sea, a sea without enough of the invisible organisms in it that he needs to keep him kicking. The life of a barnacle is threatened by

Barnacles on a rock, sweep feeding

many things we take for granted, such as hot summer sunshine, fresh water rainfalls, and frost in fall and winter. A barnacle must be able to live during the hours when the tide is out each day. He cannot move downshore when the water drops. If it is sunny, a barnacle must be able to endure the heat without being cooked inside his fortress like a crab in a pot. If it is rainy, a barnacle must not get soaked by the fresh water so unlike the sea which gives him life. Frost must not kill him before the ocean waves return to warm him up to their chill temperature. Ice is one of the greatest winter dangers to a barnacle, for its weight and sharp edges can slice him right off the rock. Except for the strength of his shell and firm attachment, he has no protection against it.

A barnacle conceals himself within walls made of a kind of limestone. It is similar to blackboard chalk, though a great deal harder. As soon as the liquid limestone leaves the barnacle and touches the water around his soft body, it hardens. He shapes a thin platform against the rough surface of the rock, locking himself to it, and around about him he makes six overlapping plates. The walls are pretty thick, considering how small a barnacle is, and they are often ridged. The infant barnacle proudly takes on adult form. He doesn't know he resembles an upside-down ice-cream cone with the point

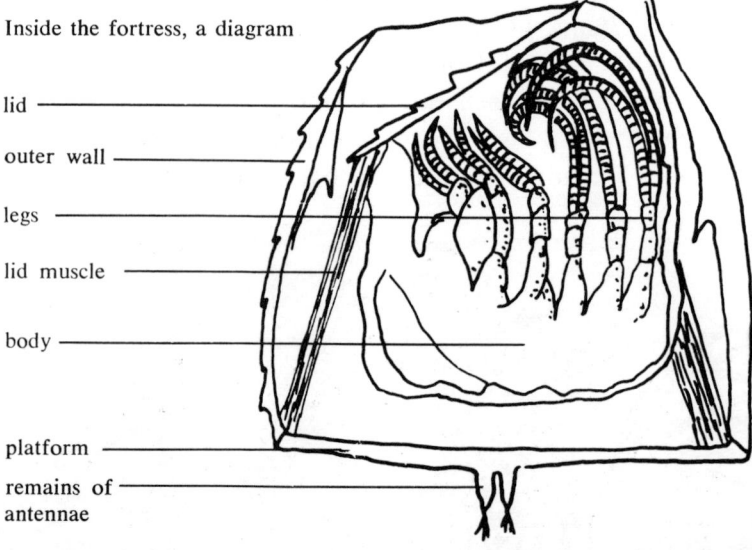

Inside the fortress, a diagram

lid

outer wall

legs

lid muscle

body

platform

remains of antennae

lopped off. Surrounded by stout walls and shut in by a lid made of four more plates, the barnacle feels secure. He can easily open and close his fortress, and stick out his legs when it seems safe to gather food. Nothing but the trap door moves, and when it closes it shuts a little bit of sea in with him each time.

A barnacle rests inside the fortress, clothed in mantle tissue like a baby in a bunting. The mantle lines all the walls making them smooth and airtight. It holds the barnacle and even shelters its developing eggs for their first four months of life. The mantle tissue makes the fortress walls, and the mantle tissue enlarges them. Somehow it dissolves the innermost layers and adds more limestone to the outside. When the limestone walls are hardened, they make the barnacle's shelter larger.

A barnacle must molt just like his relatives, the lobster and the crab, because his body also is covered with a stiff coating of chitin, which doesn't grow when the soft parts of the barnacle grow. Imagine outgrowing your own skin every now and then and having to replace it with a larger skin. A barnacle must split out of his skin and shed it from every part of him, even all the jointed sections of his long legs. He then expands the new skin which has grown underneath, and lets his body take up more room before the new skin has a chance to smooth out its wrinkles and harden. The old skin floats away into the ocean, white, transparent, a complete barnacle ghost.

The shallow, drifting waters of a spent wave entice a barnacle to kick his legs. They sweep back and forth, capturing food as by a feathery net, and kick it into his mouth. A barnacle dines on transparent plants and animals that flock through the water in fabulous numbers. They are too small for our eyes to spot, but a barnacle knows they are there, and knows exactly how to strain them out. If you have a chance one day to look at plankton beneath a microscope it would be too bad to miss the chance. You would never believe that such numbers of complete and complicated plants, mixed with numbers of energetic animals, swim in our clear ocean water. The microscopic plants are called plankton, and scores upon scores of infant animals swim among them. Many are offspring of the adult animals on shore, and many will someday become adult too. Millions of infant plants will serve as food for the animals, some of the tiny animals will eat other microscopic animals, and quantities of the plants as well as animals will become food for the creatures living along the shore.

A barnacle looks so unfamiliar that it took naturalists a long time to discover that it is related to lobsters, crabs, and other crustaceans. For years, myths took the place of facts, and many stories were told about the ship's barnacle, which is a stalked barnacle. This barnacle fastens to ships and piers by the end of a fleshy stalk, or floats around the ocean riding in clusters upside down on a

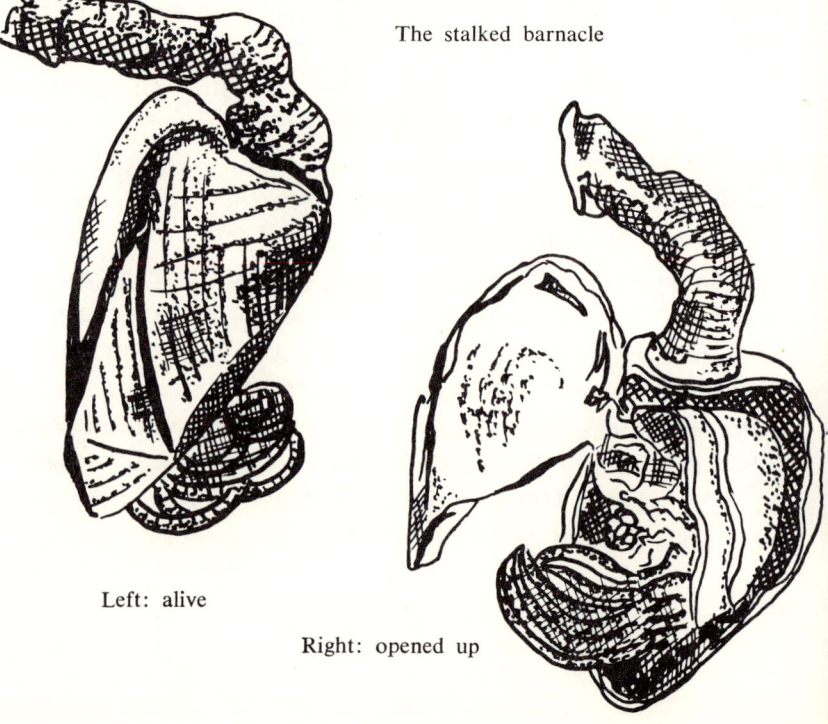

The stalked barnacle

Left: alive

Right: opened up

The barnacle tree from a fourteenth-century travel book

piece of wood. Medieval naturalists described these clusters as trees. The featherlike legs poking out of the leafy shells on the tree were thought to be the feathers of an infant domestic goose before it had taken to life on land. People smacked their lips over the barnacle geese as a delicious kind of sea food, and ate them as fish for five hundred years. Then finally it was decided that geese are meat, and fish are fish, and no goose ever spends his youth in the sea.

Of course, there is nothing surprising about this to us. We are more sophisticated than men were then and we know more about animals. These things are second nature to us now because research has made them part of general knowledge. But we have only known about barnacles since an army surgeon named John Vaughan Thompson declared he could put the barnacle in a seashore *Who's Who*. It took him quite a while, working on the problem in his spare time, to find out who are a barnacle's relatives. He first observed the habits of the shore crab, from its birth to its adult life on the rocks. He discovered that during part of its life the infant shore crab looks entirely unlike the adult. Instead of a dark-shelled, cautious crab, it was a tiny, nearly transparent larva, swimming around in the ocean plankton, eating, growing, and then molting. Each time the larva molted it looked a little more like a crab and a little less like a larva, until at last the long larval tail suddenly tucked itself under the crablike body, and the creature started living on the shore in adult fashion. When Mr. Thompson found some barnacle eggs he made the same sort of study. The infant barnacles looked exactly like the infant shore crabs, and did all of the same things. During the last few molts, the baby barnacles began to look less like shore crabs and, after the final molt, cemented themselves down by the head end and built their limestone walls.

The eyes a barnacle brings from the larval stage are quite useless inside his fortress and never develop into effective seeing organs. They probably remain as cells

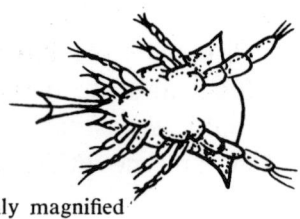

Larval barnacle, highly magnified

with some sensitivity to light. There is no heart inside the barnacle, nor any blood vessels at all. So that instead of nourishment being carried around its body by a system of veins and arteries, it passes directly into the body tissues through the walls of the stomach and intestine. From there it is spread around from cell to cell. A barnacle has

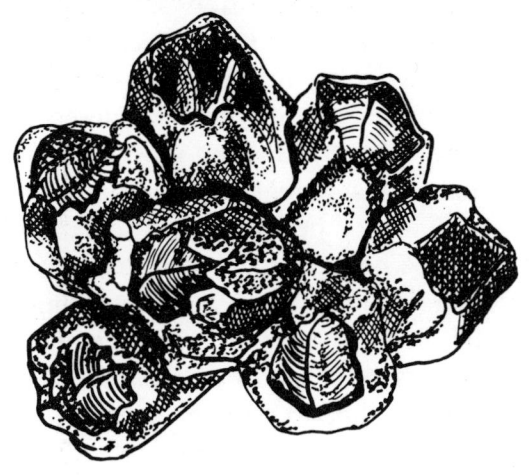

Smooth-shelled barnacles

no brain and never can think about his peculiar position upside down. But there are a few nerves near the mouth and near each of the legs, and these are all the barnacle needs to manage the business of fanning with its feet, eating with its mouth, and closing up when something disturbs it.

Because of their stout walls, barnacles seem to be lifeless shells sprinkling the rocks. But if you explore when the incoming tide begins to spray the tiny creatures you will surely change your impression. As though in happy anticipation, the barnacles open a fraction to receive the fresh salt spray. A touch on the trap door makes them close and the small muscles and little plates on top feel rather soft and springy under your finger.

A baby barnacle drifts around in the plankton on his own. And when he is ready, he chooses a spot to cement to without the help of a more mature or experienced barnacle. A barnacle may wander over the surface of a rock for an hour, trying to find a spot free of tiny plants which can make the rock very slippery. He walks up and down poking and prodding and often settling in a shallow crack. After the walls are made, he cannot ever change his mind and move away to a better spot. Even though a great deal in a barnacle's life is left to chance, a barnacle usually cements himself down no more than an inch and a half from his nearest neighbor. A barnacle doesn't settle so close to a neighbor because he is sociable. He settles this close because he must mate in order to send millions of baby barnacles into the sea each spring. Although every barnacle is both a male and a female, a barnacle cannot fertilize its own eggs. For cross-fertilization, each barnacle extends a tube to another barnacle and deposits a little sperm near the base of its legs. The developing eggs remain inside the mantle cavity of the adult barnacle for four months. While they wait to enter the ocean, the baby barnacles take shape, grow swimming legs, a pair of horns, and the barest suggestion of parts to come. After they join the plankton, they develop a pair of antennules with the ability to make cement and then a transparent

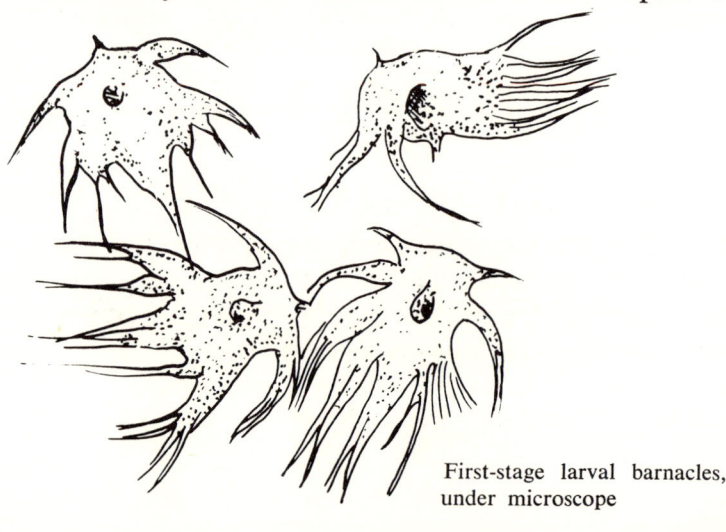

First-stage larval barnacles, under microscope

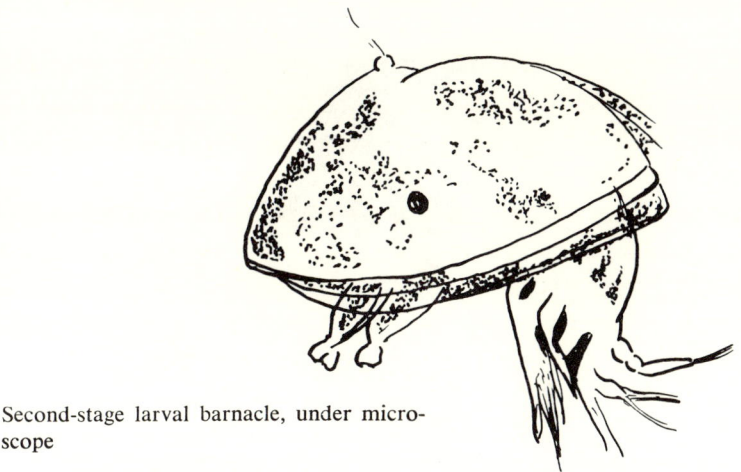

Second-stage larval barnacle, under microscope

two-piece shell. When all these changes have been made, as well as some others, the infant barnacle is ready to become an adult by a remarkable metamorphosis.

Not all barnacles are as small as acorn barnacles in the cold waters in the northern half of the world. In Chile there is another species of acorn barnacle which grows ten inches long and three or four inches wide. It makes good food. Other kinds of acorn barnacles live on turtle shells and whale hides, taking their food from the water as they are carried along. And some barnacles have given up an independent life, becoming parasites. That means they take their nourishment from the bodies of the animals they live in. Some live in crabs and some in whale

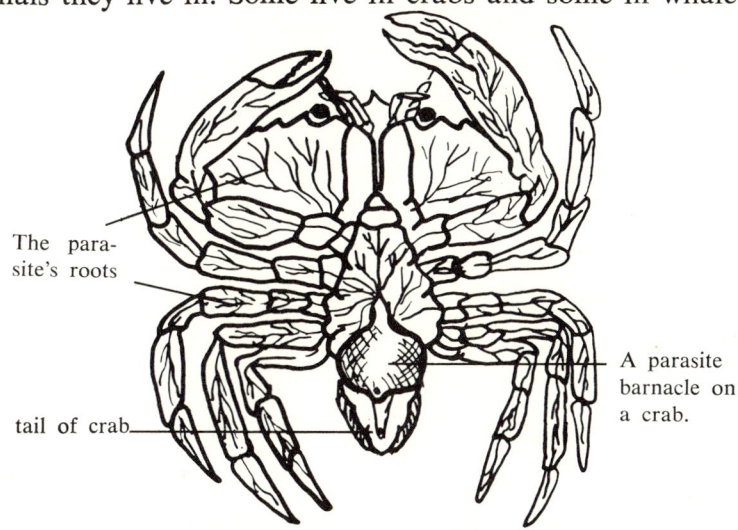

The parasite's roots

tail of crab

A parasite barnacle on a crab.

blubber. If you saw one of these parasites, you would never recognize it as a barnacle. The only time it resembles other barnacles is in the larval form.

The sea feeds the adult barnacles and plays nursemaid to their young. It gives them oxygen and it bathes them in their fortresses. The sea is the protector of the barnacle colony, but it cannot shield it from its worst enemy, the dog whelk. Dog whelks have a way of forcing open the trap doors on top and eating out the sweet meat inside. If you look carefully you will probably see some dog whelks at work.

### VOCABULARY

antennule — *a small feeler or sense organ*

crustaceans — *group of animals, called a* class *by scientists; hard shell covering soft part of body; jointed legs; most at home under water, although a bush-climbing hermit crab is an exception*

larva — *the very early form of animal that changes in body structure before it becomes adult*

metamorphosis — *the change from one form to another so that the animal looks altogether different as an adult than earlier in its life*

microscopic — *so small as to be seen only with the help of a microscope*

Tiny barnacles on a rock

A dog whelk

# THE IRRESISTIBLE RADULA

CHAPTER 2

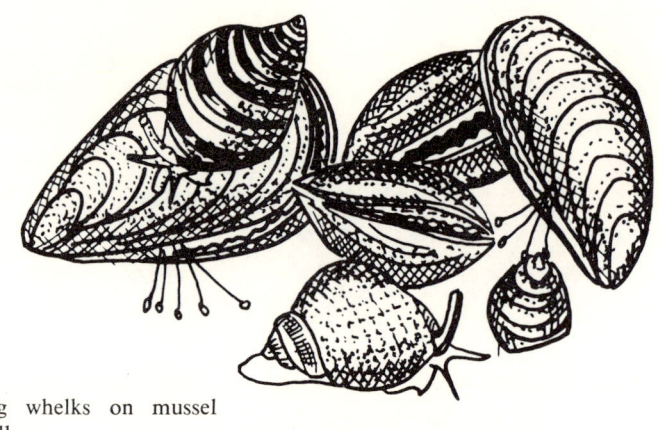

Dog whelks on mussel shells

The dog whelk is a carnivorous snail. This means that he eats meat rather than vegetables or, to put it plainly, he eats mussels or barnacles but not seaweed of any size or variety. If barnacles or mussels are not there, the dog whelk still won't starve. He will begin to devour the soft parts of limpets, small periwinkles, and other kinds of snails. The dog whelk sounds like a ferocious and resourceful animal, but when you see him on the rocks he looks like nothing of the sort. He shows you his back, and moves slowly, or doesn't move at all. There are no gleaming eyes to show you he is full of mischief, no snarl to indicate his malice. There is no stalking, no struggle. A dog whelk just moves quietly along, gobbling up helpless animals underneath him.

Barnacles are strong and can protect themselves against many dangers. But they cannot resist the dog whelk, who is so much larger and can cover a whole barnacle with its foot. No one can see what happens beneath that foot, although we know how the dog whelk eats. When the whelk has moved away the barnacle is gone. The dog whelk may have secreted a substance called purpurin to kill or put the barnacle to sleep. Then with the resistance gone from the muscles commanding the barnacle's trap door, the dog whelk extends his proboscis and rasps out his meal with a special tongue. The bits of barnacle disappear into the dog whelk's mouth.

The dog whelk has a harder time eating mussels than barnacles because the shells are larger and tougher, but these difficulties don't really bother him. He climbs up onto the shell and with his radula, which is the name for his special tongue, he bores a very neat round hole right through the mussel's shell. After that there is nothing to do but eat up the mussel. Probably if you could ask the dog whelk he would say he preferred baby mussels to any other food. They don't have to be drilled; they can be forced open and eaten just like the barnacles, and they provide a much richer meal.

While dog whelks are busy eating up a barnacle colony, young mussels have a chance to land and settle, undisturbed, on the shore. They grow peacefully until the dog whelks have ravished the barnacles and begin to

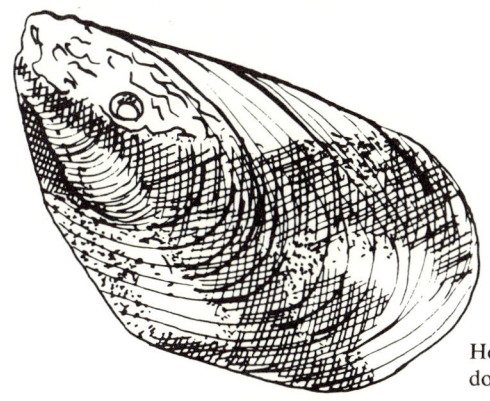

Horse mussel bored by dog whelk

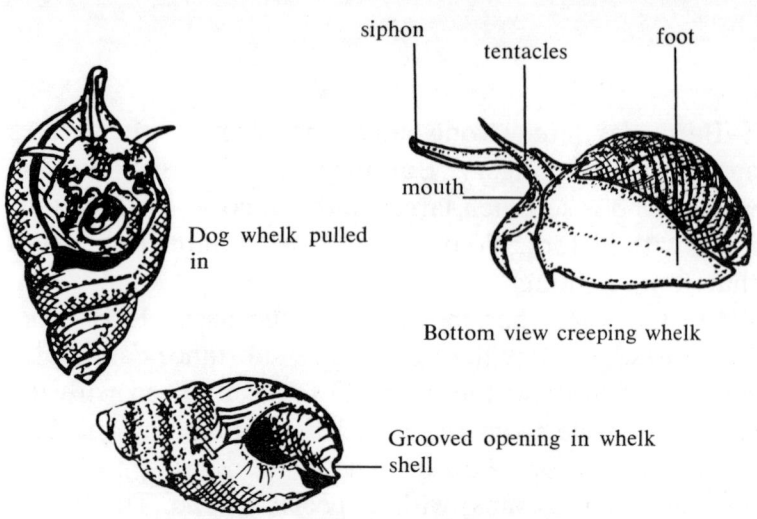

creep over to find food in the mussel beds. At first the dog whelks don't know how to get at the mussels. Sometimes they drill holes in empty shells, working from inside out, or outside in. Finally they discover the shells of living mussels and unerringly drill into them. After a time some of the whelk shells, which were white while the creatures ate barnacles, begin to take on some purple-black stripes, telling tales of their new diet of mussels.

Carnivorous snails were not the first living things to colonize the shoreline rocks. Plants appeared there first, for plants are self-sufficient, and depend on no other creatures for food. They can take the chemicals their bodies need directly from the sea, and then, using the energy of sunlight, they can fashion the substances they have drawn from the water into living body tissue. Animals always have depended on plants for the nourishment their bodies need. Either they eat the plants themselves, or they eat other animals that have eaten plants. Some animals, like ourselves, eat both plants and plant-eating animals. So that the first animals to live on the rocks were herbivorous creatures, using the plants for food, and sometimes for shelter as well. Then when the plant eaters became numerous, the carnivorous snails came to feed on them.

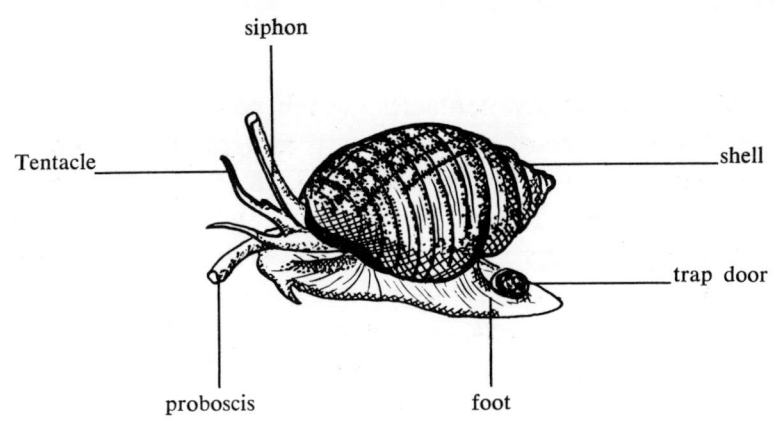

Scientists think that the dog whelk first grew accustomed to life on a sandy or muddy bottom and later settled on the rocks. There with much the same body he learned to lead a new life. Each dog whelk, in a piece of folded tissue that extends as a tube over his head, carries evidence that his ancestors lived differently. The tube is called a siphon. If the snail once moved through sandy or muddy water the siphon would reach the clear water above. A dog whelk on the rocks has no problems obtaining clear water, and for life there the siphon is not a necessity. Perhaps some day nature will forget to reproduce it, and a young dog whelk will be born without a siphon. A dog whelk uses clean water for breathing by passing it through a small chamber filled with tiny, thin leaves of tissue. The water passes among the gills, and of course they must remain clean. If a little mud were brought in they would become clogged up and the dog whelk would die. Another kind of whelk still lives on muddy bottoms, and still uses the siphon to fetch in clear water. This whelk, whose proper name is Buccinum Undatum, has a much longer, and more useful, siphon than his cousin, the dog whelk.

Under the spiral shell with its siphon groove you can see some of the soft part of the whelk. There is the muscular foot which supports the shell and moves it along by a series of contractions. There is the stumpy head with odd-looking hollow tentacles, which can be pulled into the head in case of danger. Nerve centers are located in the head for the discovery of food, in the foot for protection against danger, and near the gill chamber and intestine to keep them operating perfectly. There are simple eyes which feel light and shadow. In times of trouble, the dog whelk has one standard reaction. A long muscle that stretches back into the smallest section of the spiral pulls the snail into his shell and closes him

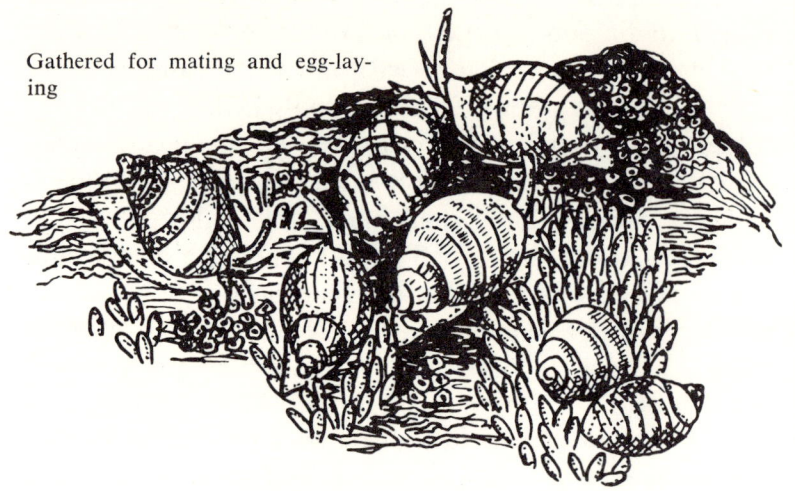

Gathered for mating and egg-laying

mostly in by shutting the operculum. The strong, important muscle is called the columnella. The operculum is made of a horny material similar to our fingernails. It is very tough, and the more you pry at the opening of the shell trying to get at the snail, the farther in the columnella draws it. A dog whelk grows as big as his diet will let him within a certain range of sizes, and then when he is sexually mature he stops growing altogether and the shell thickens up and the opening becomes grooved. It is possible for young dog whelks to be larger than the older mature ones, if they have had an easier time getting

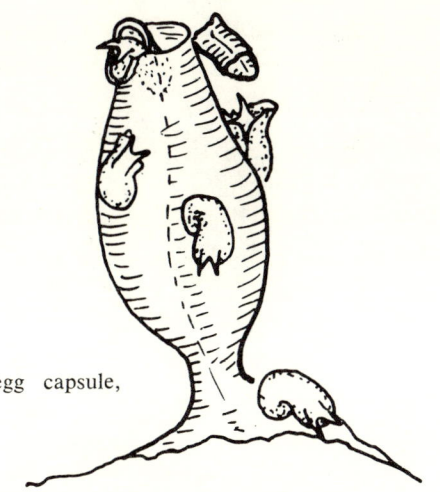

Young whelks leaving ripe egg capsule, drawn very large

food on the rocks, but all dog whelks eventually stop growing. This is unlike the periwinkles who grow all their lives, even if by our standards they never get very large. It is not hard to tell a dog whelk from a common periwinkle. You must simply look for the ridges and grooves along the opening in the dog whelk shell, and the round smoothness of the opening in the periwinkle.

When they are mature, dog whelks gather in rock crevices to mate. They may do this at any time of year, but they generally get together in the winter. They are a cold-blooded animal, changing body temperature with the weather and the water. You couldn't say they have their loves to keep them warm, but they search out the other dog whelks in the cracks and there the females lay little yellow capsules, the size and shape of grains of wheat. These are securely fastened to the rocks in case of winter storms. One dog whelk lays about thirty-six capsules at a spawning, and in a whole year may lay as many as two hundred. Each capsule holds many, many eggs but not all of them possess the ability to develop. Most of the eggs serve as food for about twelve infant snails that take

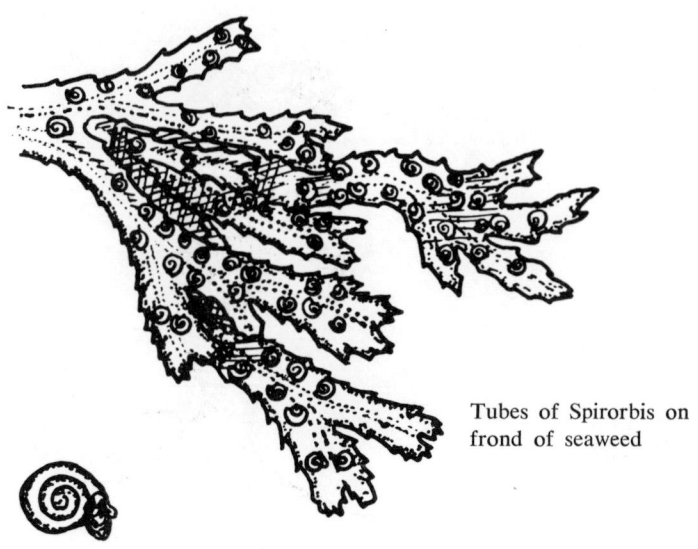

Tubes of Spirorbis on frond of seaweed

One tube magnified

shape from twelve fertile eggs. The infants stay inside eating eggs for about four months. Then the capsule turns purple and from the inside come twelve tiny dog whelks, ready to adopt all the habits of their parents. A baby dog whelk is a frail creature and the water immediately carries it downshore to feed on a worm that lives in a limestone tube lying in a flat coil on the surface of seaweeds. Spirorbis is a small worm living in a delicate stone house, and young dog whelks learn the art of drilling on these little tubes.

The shell on the back of a young dog whelk has barely taken a complete turn around when he emerges from the wheat-colored egg case. But as the flesh of Spirorbis fills his intestine and puts his digestive gland hard to work, the dog whelk begins to grow. The digestive gland grows, and the snail grows, and the digestive gland grows some more. If the digestive gland grew in regular fashion it would soon lie behind the snail on the rock, and trail

18

around after him in a most awkward manner. But the digestive gland doesn't grow in a normal fashion. It grows long on one side, and stays short on the other, and before you know it, it is twisting around into a spiral. Then covered by the one-piece shell which a snail makes with a special part of his body, the spiral remains there always, and instead of a trailing intestine the snail carries his enormous digestive gland neatly balanced over his foot. The shell is later enlarged by adding onto the opening. A spiral shell is very compact and goes easily where the snail goes, up and down rock crevices, over the edges of the mussel shells. The shell protects the snail from injury when it is washed around the rocks by waves, for a dog whelk is not always particular about hiding in a crack. And if it is left on a rock by a lowering tide, the dog whelk pulls himself down. He is a careless creature and doesn't hide himself inside as completely as a periwinkle. Still, a little air seems to do his tough flesh no harm, and he lives very happily on the rocks.

### VOCABULARY

carnivorous — *meat-eating*
digestive gland — *a mass of tissue which produces chemicals to aid the snail in digesting meat*
herbivorous — *plant-eating*
proboscis — *trunk-like extension of head protruded through the mouth opening.*
purpurin — *a purple dye made by the body of the dog whelk with perhaps a drugging effect on some animals. Once used to dye cloth and called Tyrhhian purple*
radula — *a coiled tongue the dog whelk sends out through his mouth*

Change of diet can produce stripes

Baby mussels on seaweed

# HANGING BY A THREAD

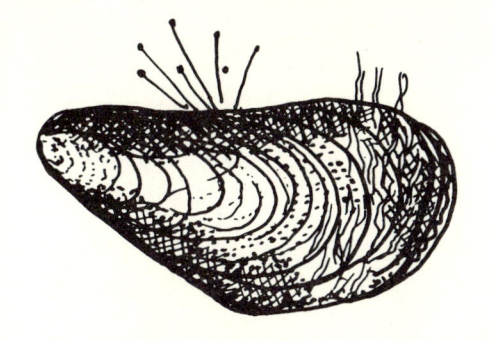

CHAPTER 3

Mussels hardly look like animals, and when you see them literally covering a shore, fastened to the rocks in huge blue bunches, you can scarcely imagine that they are alive. They have hard shells which are made by the infant mussels when they are little more than tiny transparent creatures. The shells are enlarged by a special fold of skin inside and grow about an inch a year if conditions are good. Conditions are usually not good, for mussels come to the shore in enormous numbers, and after attaching themselves must wait for food to come to them in the waves. Usually there are too many mussels, and they are so crowded on the shore that they never get enough food, or enough space, to grow very fast.

If you sit on a rock at the shore and watch the mussels lying around at your feet, they will not move. The only thing you will notice, perhaps, is a tiny rim of brown flesh, ruffled, and yet hardly apparent between the two "valves." This means that the mussel is open and is busy straining food out of the water. In the summer when the ocean waters feel warm compared to their temperature in winter, each mussel may strain six glassfuls of water an hour through its barely opened shell.

Look around you closely and you will see a lot of very small mussels among the larger ones. If you pull one of these away, snapping and tearing dozens of thin brown threads off the rocks, you can put it in a glass of sea water. It is possible then, after some time has gone by and the mussel feels safe, to watch him slowly hoist himself up the side of the glass, pulling on threads he makes with his light tan foot. By tedious effort he makes threads, attaches them higher on the side of the glass every time, and pulls off the ones below him, dragging himself up bit by bit. At long last the mussel we never believed could move at all has reached the top. The top for him is not the rim of the glass but the surface of the water. The water line is his place in nature too, and despite waves and undertow he works his way up along the shore by his byssus threads. When the tide drops, the mussel does not move down the shore again; he closes up and waits through the period between tides.

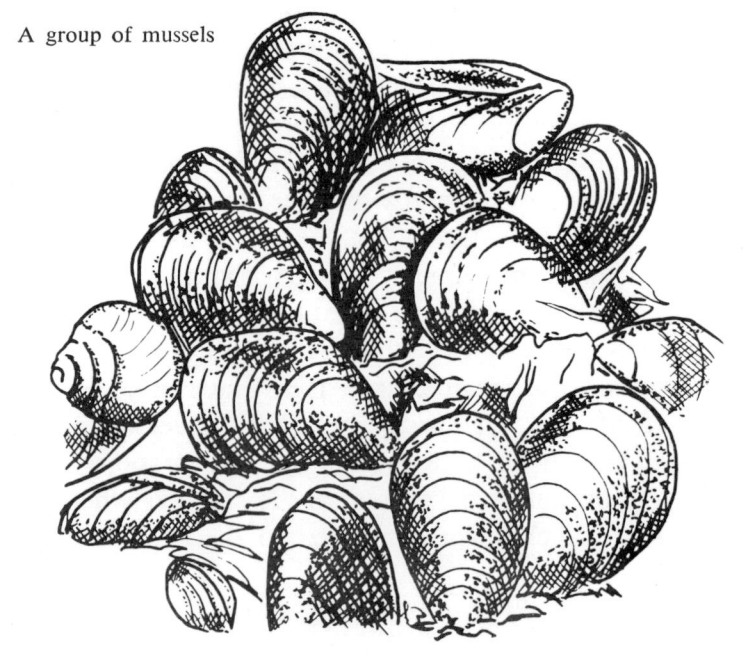

A group of mussels

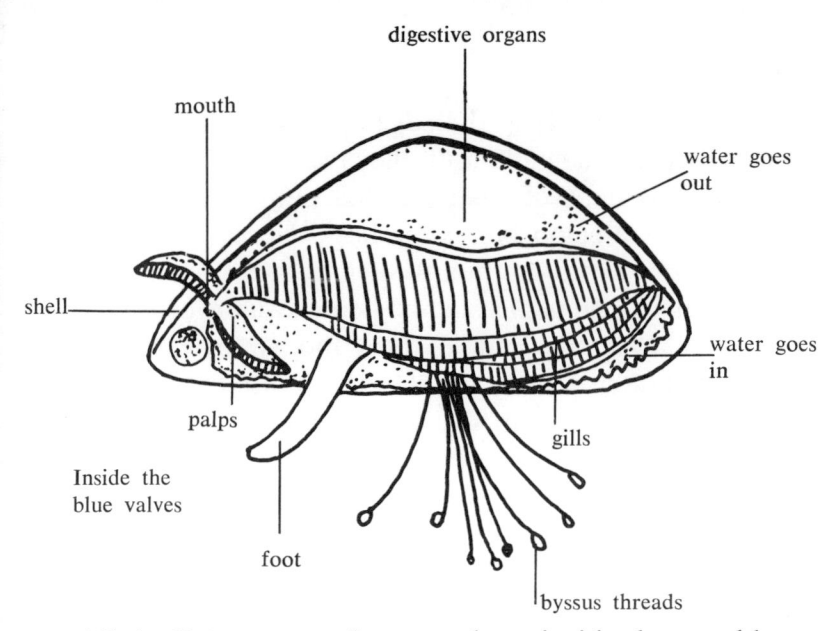

Diagram labels: digestive organs, mouth, water goes out, shell, water goes in, palps, gills, Inside the blue valves, foot, byssus threads

All the living parts of a mussel are inside the two blue valves fastened together with a hinge. The hinge is near the narrow end of the mussel, where inside is hidden a mouth without a head to go around it. Mussels are headless creatures, and since the end with the mouth cannot be called the head end, it is called the anterior. The anterior of the mussel faces the waves when the surf is high, and because it is so narrow the water flows easily around it, and the waves don't bang the life out of the animal. The wide end opens and shuts when the mussel wants it to, and when he relaxes his muscles, the shell opens a little, and water flows in from the sea. Water flows in because of the waving motion of multitudes of tiny hairs, called cilia. The cilia direct the water through the gills, which strain from the floating plankton everything small enough to make a meal. And while the filaments are straining the food, the mantle is taking oxygen from the flowing water. At low tide a mussel closes, and water, food, and oxygen are stored inside him to keep him going until he is covered by the sea again. The bits of food are packed into neat bundles with mucus made by the gills, and off they go along the edges of the gill filaments, always by the same path, until they reach the mouth. At the mouth two flaps of tissue, called palps, cast aside the pieces that are too big. Very large pieces would choke the mussel. From the mouth of a mussel food goes into the stomach and is digested by being swallowed up whole by cells. Ordinary animals turn food into watery combinations of chemicals and these pass into the cells of the digestive tract. But in the mussel the walls of the intestine take in the tiny pieces whole, so the palps allow only the smallest pieces to go through the mussel's mouth.

It's strange to say that a mussel doesn't have a head, although he has a mouth, but he really would have no use for one and presumably that's why it isn't there. But although he can't be said to run around, he has, and needs, a foot. It is the foot which contains a gland to make threads which hold the mussel firmly to the rocks. It is the foot which places the threads expertly, so that they can stand the strain of the waves. When the old byssus threads break, the foot discretely emerges from within to secrete new threads and fasten them to the rocks. Some threads go forward, some backward, enough in each direction to hold no matter which way the water rushes. If the mussel bed is in a location where some mud settles down on top of the animals, the foot is able to lengthen the threads so that the shells again rest on top of the mud. Generally mussel beds are so tightly packed that each mussel loses the ability to move at all. You even wonder how they can open. But where the animals do not live so closely quartered, and there is a reason to go, the mussel's foot can carry him slowly along to a better location, perhaps a place with more food. A mussel can sometimes go

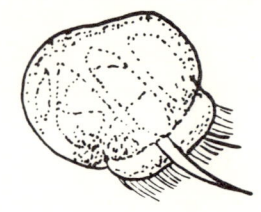

Larval mussel magnified

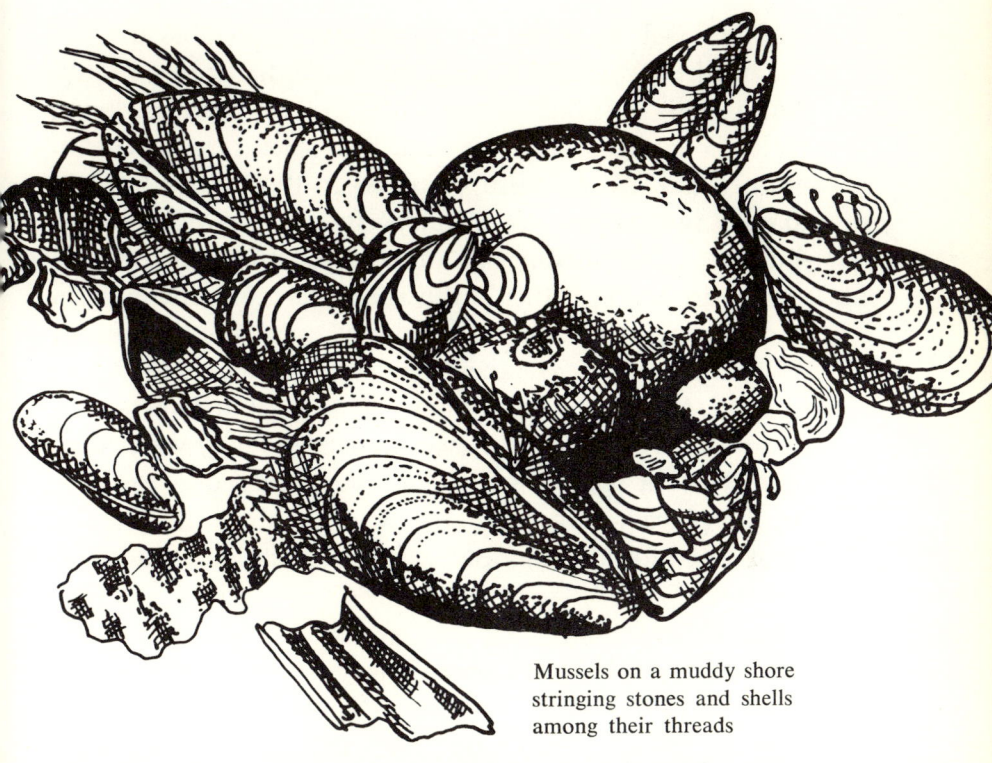

Mussels on a muddy shore stringing stones and shells among their threads

short distances, but the foot manages it only with some difficulty and is not able to carry the mussel away from the dangerous dog whelks, or starfish, or human beings, that threaten him.

Female mussels release millions of eggs into the sea water at spawning times, and somehow, as soon as the eggs are drifting in the waves, the male mussels know it is time to release their millions upon millions of male cells. For convenience the millions of male cells are called milt. The milt surrounds the eggs and soon each egg is entered by one, but only one, male cell. This union is a spark of energy to the male and female cells. They cannot live alone, but once they come together they divide and develop into a completely new individual. With mussels there is not much chance for variation and the baby mussel looks just like its parents, who look just like each other. Within twelve hours after the union, the dividing cells are able to swim through the water by waving cilia. Some time later the cilia become a flapping membrane, and this too disappears when the foot and transparent two-piece shell develop. By this time the infant mouth, and stomach. The time has come for the mussel comes in contact. Inside the shell are miniature gills, a mouth, and stomach. The time has come for the mussel to find the rocks. It takes some time to look around. It walks over seaweed on its foot, and under the surface of the water. Gradually it moves up near the high water line, and the foot starts making the byssus threads. It is now in the place where it will spend most of its life, eating, growing, reproducing, and trying to resist its enemies.

VOCABULARY

anterior — *the end that faces forward, in this case toward the waves*
cilia — *microscopic moving hairs*
valves — *name given to two-pieced shells of clams, mussels, scallops, etc*

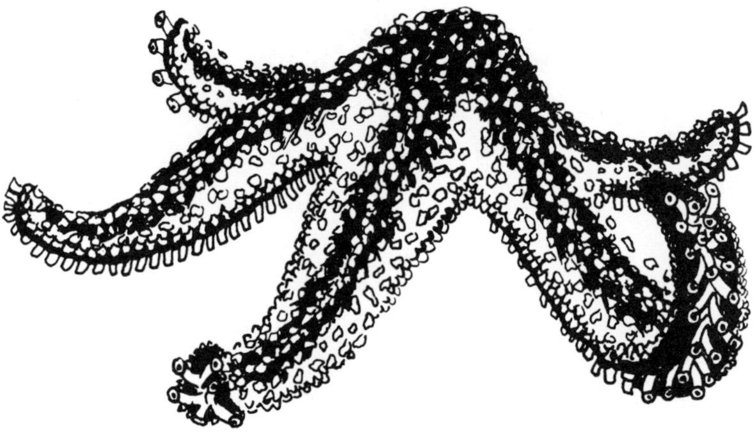

# A CLOSE AND DEADLY EMBRACE

CHAPTER 4

An arm

Long ago when men first began to culture pearls in oyster beds, starfish turned up and threatened to eat up all the oysters and ruin all the half-formed pearls. An oyster makes a pearl by depositing thin pearl layers around a grain of sand. Each year the oyster secretes another layer, and the pearl becomes a little larger. But starfish care nothing for pearls. They only want to eat the shellfish that make them. So the pearl growers sent for divers, and the divers pulled starfish from the oysterbeds by the hundreds. Men on the docks ripped the starfish to pieces and when they were finished threw the whole lot of them back into the sea. Such brutal treatment would have killed another kind of animal but not the starfish. In a few months many of the pieces that had been thrown in had grown into nearly complete, new animals, and for each starfish that had been eating oysters before, there were now two or three new starfish stuffing themselves.

Oyster fishermen learned about regeneration the hard way. Because they didn't know that starfish can grow new parts when they lose the old ones, they lost hundreds of oysters. Fortunately, not every piece of a broken starfish can grow a whole new self around about it. Usually there has to be a good portion of the central disc and an arm remaining, or the lone section of starfish dies. When you find a starfish with just an arm, a central disc and four arm buds, you have found a comet star, that is, a regenerating starfish.

Whether you call the five, pointed, mobile sections of a starfish arms, or whether you call them legs, depends on your point of view. I don't think a shellfish fisherman would hesitate in answering, *arms*! All he is concerned with is how to loosen the deadly and insistent embrace of the starfish from the shells of the oysters, clams, mussels, or scallops that he collects and sells.

Starfish are gluttons. They eat enormously, and they eat rather efficiently. They can grow very large on their diet. They have strong arms and suckers, and a special stomach for eating extra large animals. A multitude of tube feet run in pairs down a groove on the lower side of each arm. Each tube foot has a sucker which can be attached to anything a starfish desires, and released when-

A broken starfish, growing two new arms

A starfish eating a mussel

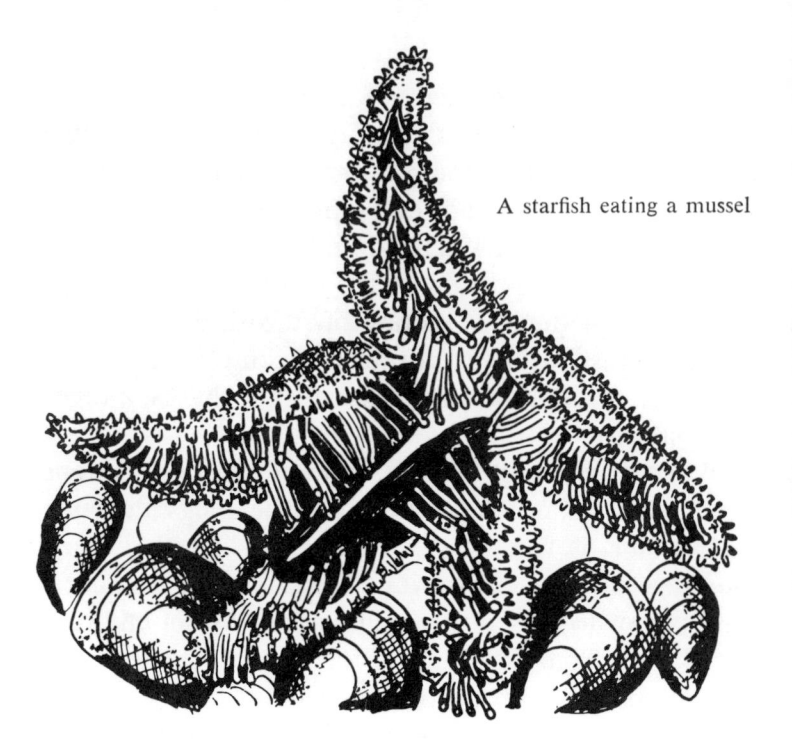

ever he wishes. When a starfish eats a mussel he wraps himself around the shell gripping each valve with the suckers of one arm. He pulls and the mussel counters the attack by closing tightly and staying closed. But the mussel tires out easily, and yields a little under the strain. The mussel's shell opens a slight bit, and that narrow opening is plenty for the starfish. Some say he injects some poison and destroys the mussel's determination to resist. No one is sure about what happens, except that little by little the mussel gives way, and soon the starfish is digesting him. The starfish doesn't pull the mussel out of his shell to eat him. He doesn't take the mussel into his stomach through his mouth. Instead he rolls his large sack-like stomach out and digests the mussel right within the mussel's shell. This is a handy method, because a starfish has no way to make a large piece of food smaller except by covering it with his stomach and digesting it where it lies. Later he can finish up a few small fragments by pulling them, and his stomach, inside. Digestive juices are sent to the stomach from glands in each arm, and nutrition from the food is stored in the arms for times when food becomes scarce. Waste is passed out the anus on the top side.

A starfish doesn't find his food by looking for it, because he has no eyes. All he can do is feel whether it is sunny or dark by turning the small sensitive red spots on the ends of his arms upwards. He feels the light on these arm tips in a way similar to the way we feel the sun on our eyelids when lying on our backs outside. But he does have some other sensory equipment to help him out in his blind search. Some of his tube feet are sensitive to smells in the water, and all of them, as well as his terminal tentacle, are sensitive to touch. His skin too has tiny hairs that can be seen under a microscope, and sensory cells to help find food and warn him against danger.

Starfish live on the rocks but they hide from the waves when the sea is rough. They stay under rocks, and seaweed and in some of the quieter tidal pools. They need to find shelter from the rough water because they can be easily washed away. Starfish are not attached like the barnacles and cannot hold themselves to the rocks when the ocean is rushing swiftly in and out. A starfish hides

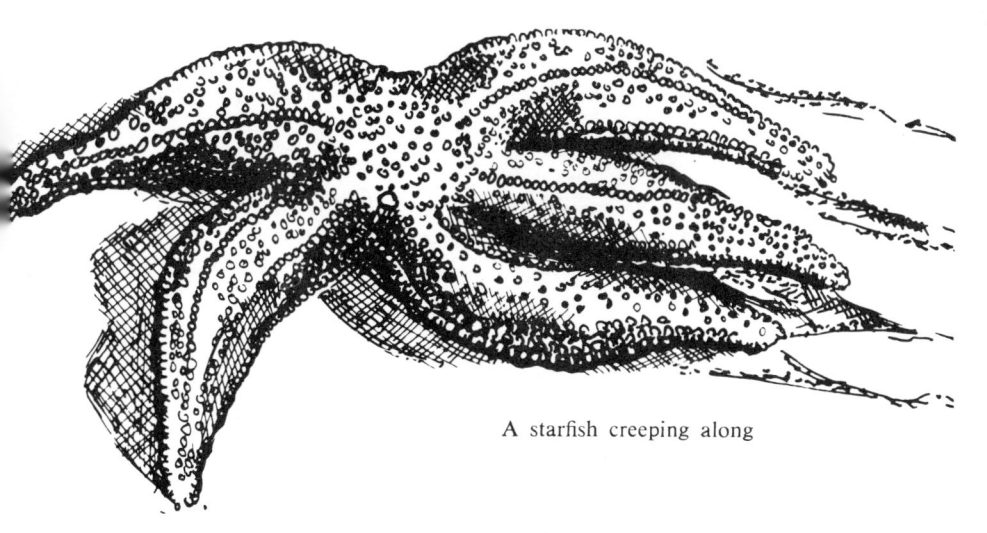

A starfish creeping along

not from fear of being broken or torn, although it is an inconvenience to lose an arm or half a body. He hides to keep from being thrown into dry or tide-deserted rocks where he would die. A starfish is completely dependent on the sea. Without water his body collapses, like a balloon without air. The important difference is that, once a starfish collapses, he can never be blown up again.

His tube feet are operated from within by water pressure. The suckers extend or retract, depending on what messages the nerves send the muscles of the water system inside. When the starfish gets the signal, the tube feet of one arm are extended and the suckers are made to stick to the rock. Then the muscles of the other arms move them up close to the "head" arm, and the suckers on these arms are made to stick also. The "head" arm then stretches out again, and the suckers drag it a little way forward. And so the starfish makes his slow way along the rock.

Without water the starfish couldn't move, and he also could no longer breathe! In between the spines and pincers are little flaps of skin filled with fluid coming from the inside of the starfish. These are gills, and you will see them near the center on the top of the arms. They are the oxygen gatherers for the starfish. Oxygen in the water moves through the membranes into the fluid inside, and from there is spread throughout the body of the animal. The oxygen serves as fuel for all the body cells and gives

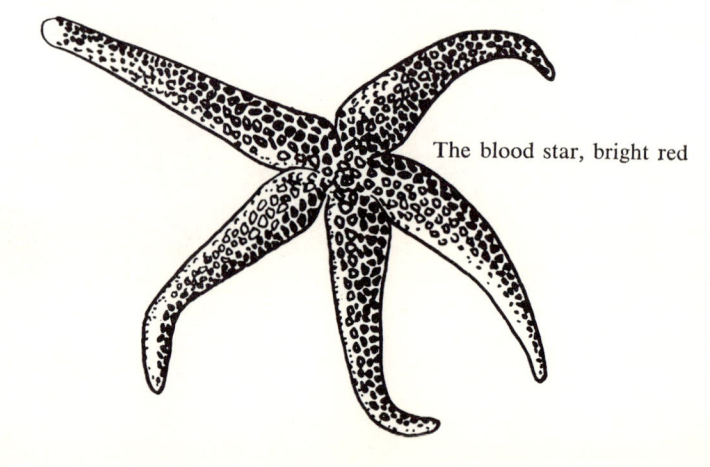

The blood star, bright red

*What's in an arm*

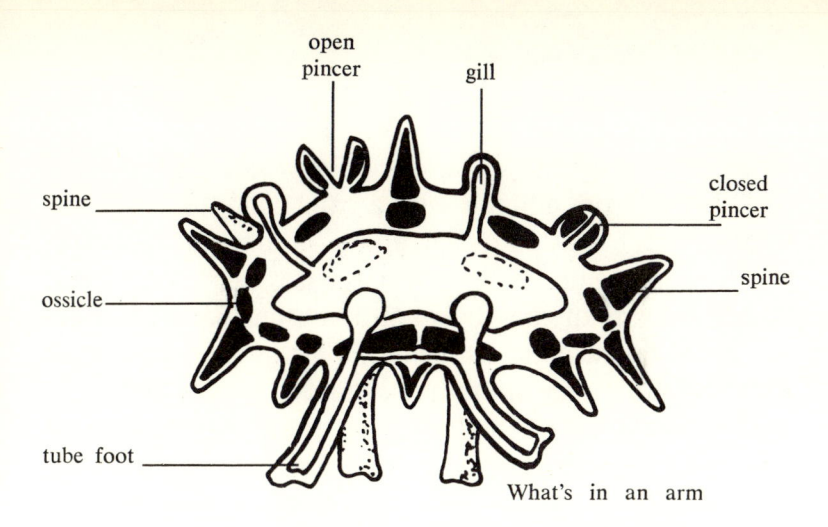

them the energy to carry out their various jobs. Oxygen and food are carried to muscles and nerves, sense organs and reproductive organs in water the starfish has taken from the sea for his own use. Everything a starfish needs is in the ocean. Out of it there is nothing for him, no food, no water, and none of the messages he must respond to in order to live and reproduce.

When the season comes for the male and female starfish to cast their eggs or sperm into the sea, there is a chemical signal which tells all the starfish that it is time to spawn. They all spawn at once and the eggs and sperm unite and develop into small larvae. The larvae swim around the sea, propelling themselves along by a waving band of microscopic hairs. They change form a number of times, each one known to scientists by a different name, and then at last, they grow three parts in the mouth area which can fasten them to shore line objects. The little

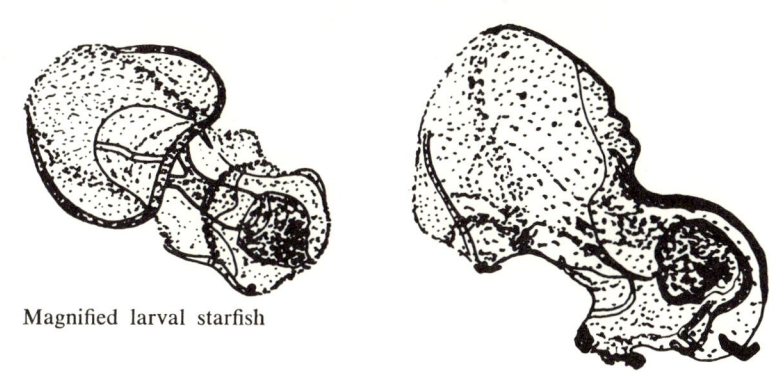

Magnified larval starfish

larvae attach themselves to rocks or weeds on the shore and change from animals with a front (mouth) end, and a rear (anal) end, a top side and a bottom side, into animals whose underneath side possesses the mouth and whose top side the anus, and all the other parts are located in a circle around the center. This huge change from bilateral symmetry to radial symmetry is called metamorphosis. It is as complicated as the metamorphosis of a butterfly, and the animal you see finally is very interesting, even if it lacks the grace and beauty of a butterfly. A starfish sometimes is a marvelous red, orange, lavender, or blue-green. Its upper-surface texture is neither all soft nor all hard, because mixed with the flesh are many ossicles or tiny limestone plates, and many spines, and tiny hard pincers, which are like little pliers and are called pedicellariae. Every piece of stone helps protect the starfish, and together they function as something of a skeleton. For if he did not have these stony pieces throughout him to harden up his body he would be like gelatine, and couldn't move himself around at all. The pincers serve the important function of keeping the arms of the starfish clean. And they are also useful underneath his arms to protect the soft tube feet and nerves. Whenever tiny bits of seaweed, seaside animals, or bits of sand settle down

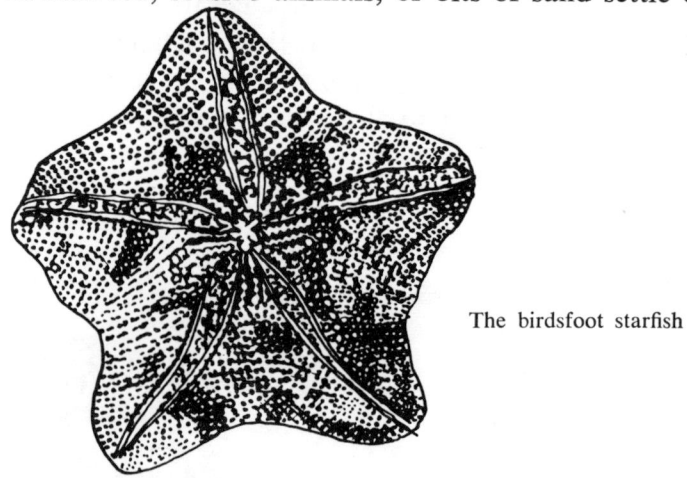

The birdsfoot starfish

between the spines, the pincers are there to clean the starfish up again. They pick up the unwanted litter and dump it off into the sea water again. This is why the starfish is clean, neat, and presentable when we inspect him on the shore.

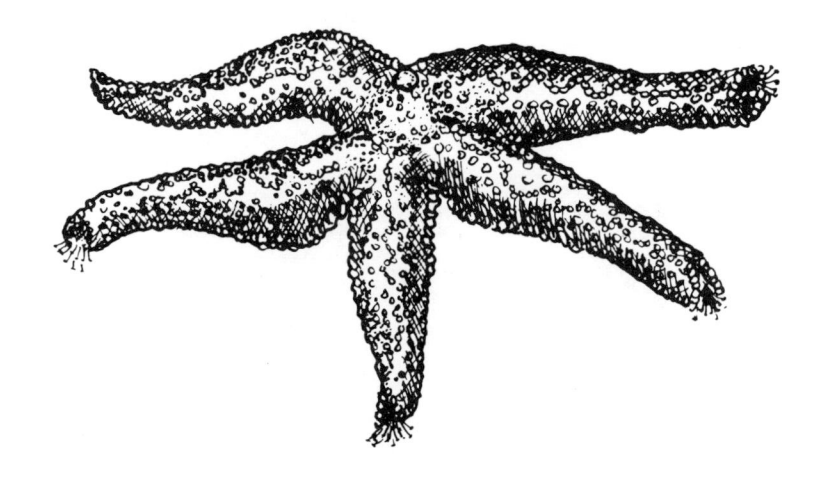

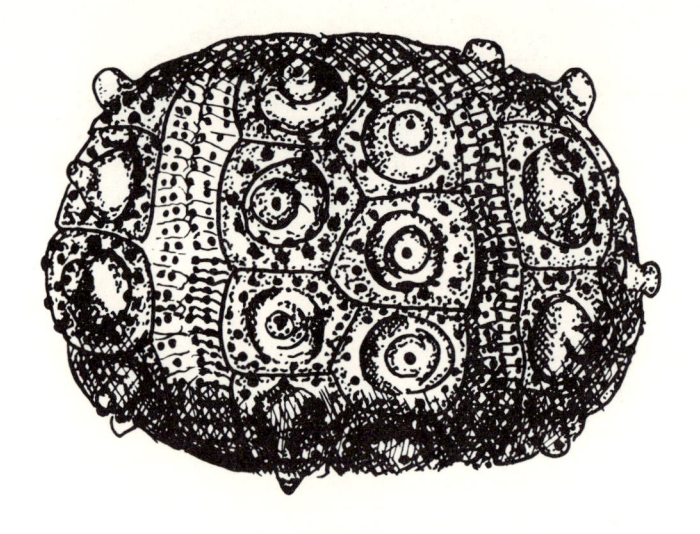

Test of tropical urchin

# SEA URCHINS

CHAPTER 5

Hobbling along like a chubby little youngster on stilts, the sea urchin makes his way in and out of the weed-covered cracks, and around under the stones of the shore. Although his spines are not long enough or sharp enough to hurt you when you pick him up, there are a great many of them. It is not the body of the urchin that you hold in your hand so cautiously, but the tips of the spines. I remember holding the cold, prickling spines of the gray-green creature as a child. It was not very big, no more than an inch and a half across, and although I could somehow sense its life, it never grew less rigid in my hand. As long as I held it, it remained frozen. Then when it was free and safe again, the spines recovered their life and mobility. It was a great treat to me to discover a crack full of different-sized urchins. I returned again and again and still found them there, just under the surface of a shallow pool and wedged tightly into a rock crevice.

A small green urchin

Sea urchins eat the tiniest plants growing on the walls of cracks, between rocks and under stones, where they hide. At every high tide they are newly free to find food in the open. It seems that urchins hide in cracks to protect themselves from the sea gulls, which bounce and hop all over the rocks along the shore trying to find them. Sea urchins are food for gulls in America. For some reason Americans have never learned to enjoy them, and certainly I would rather study an urchin than eat it myself. But taste for a food is largely a matter of habit and in Europe the rocks are scoured for urchins to eat. It's said they are delicious.

The spines and body skeleton, called the test, of the sea urchin look very much like the hard outer covering on lobsters, crabs, barnacles, and the insects that we know on land. All of the arthropods have a chitinous substitute for bones which covers their whole body like a brittle skin. It's called an exoskeleton. But although the test of the sea urchin covers the soft inner organs it is not the outermost layer of its body. Over the test, and each and every spine, is a thin layer of soft skin called the epidermis, which crabs and barnacles do not have. Usually it wears off the spines of the sea urchin, and that is why we are fooled into thinking that it is not there.

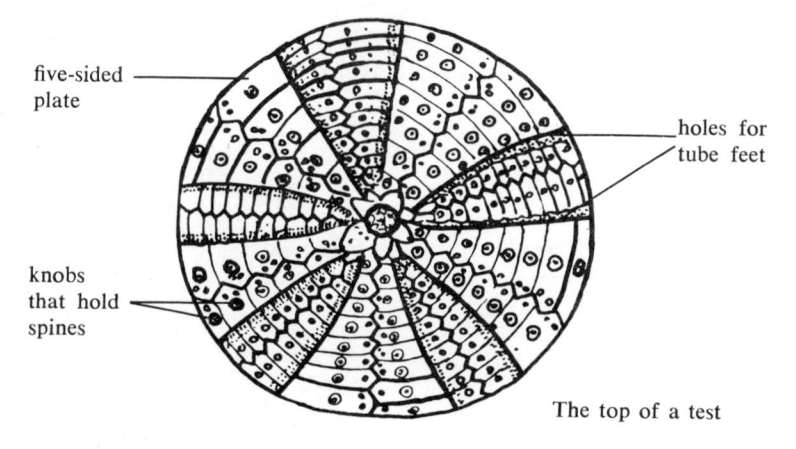

five-sided plate

holes for tube feet

knobs that hold spines

The top of a test

tube foot

tooth

spine

mouth

The underside of a living urchin

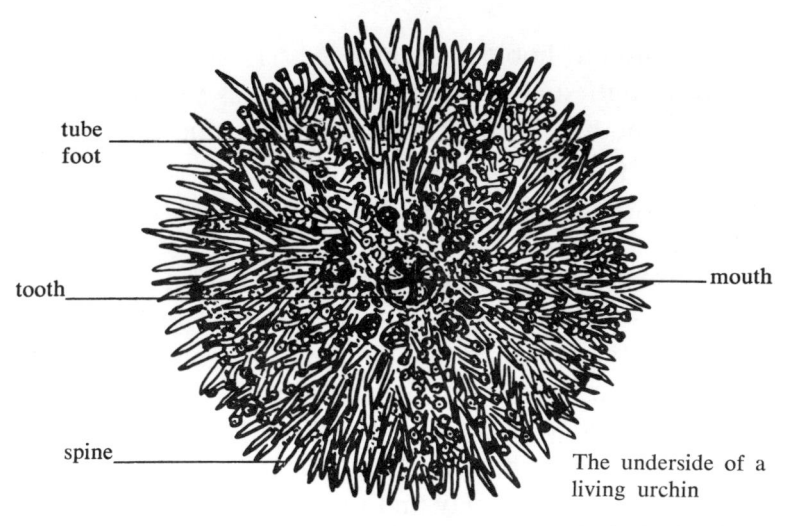

    Each spine rests on a little knob with a hole in it. You can see the knobs if you look closely at a living urchin, but you can see them better on the test of a dead and dry sea urchin that has had its spines scraped off. The hole in the center of each knob, or boss, is there for a very good reason. Muscles pass through each opening and move the spines about. These are the muscles which freeze the spines when we hold an urchin in our hands, after tearing him from his hiding place. And these are the spines which discourage his enemies, with the exception of the sea gulls and you and me. Common sea urchins do have sharp spines, but they are not dangerous.

    In deep warm seas there lives an urchin which we cannot handle. It is an alert creature and quickly detects objects in the water nearby. Immediately it rotates all its spines until their poisonous tips are dangerously pointed at the enemy. And then beware, for its spines carry a virulent poison. If the object moves, the spines follow it defensively. This tropical urchin can depend on itself without constantly hiding in cracks and sticking there with the suction cups on its tube feet. It hobbles around the ocean bottom unafraid.

A sea urchin hobbles because he has no legs, and he uses his mouth and spines as crutches. His tube feet with their sucker tips hold him to the rocks, and this is appropriate because his mouth is underneath, and must be close to the rocks in order to bite off breakfast, lunch, and supper.

An urchin's mouth has such a special design that it has been given a name to show how beautiful and complicated an organ it is. It is lantern-shaped and has been named after a famous Greek philosopher whose involved ideas are wonderful yet also puzzling. It is called Aristotle's Lantern. If you are lucky enough to find an urchin test on the shore, you may find the remains of a mouth inside. When you pull it out you'll find it feels as hard as bone. It is made of various kinds of hardened calcium, and when the urchin is alive there are muscles attached to all the movable rods and parts. Five teeth poke out of the urchin and bite tiny plants off the rocks. Five jaws inside hold one tooth each. Muscles running this way and that move the teeth, making them go in and out, in and out.

Besides chewing plants from the rocks, the mouth pumps water inside, and from the hollow in the lantern sends the water into the gills. Some urchins have gills on the inside of the body. Some have them on the outside. The thin-skinned tube feet help the gills as oxygen gatherers. A different kind of urchin, called the heart urchin, lives in holes on sandy beaches and has especially long tube feet made just for "breathing." The gills take oxygen

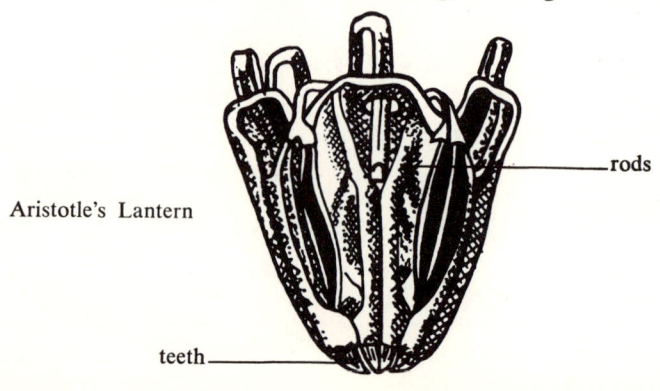

Aristotle's Lantern

rods

teeth

Heart urchin extending tube-feet "gills"

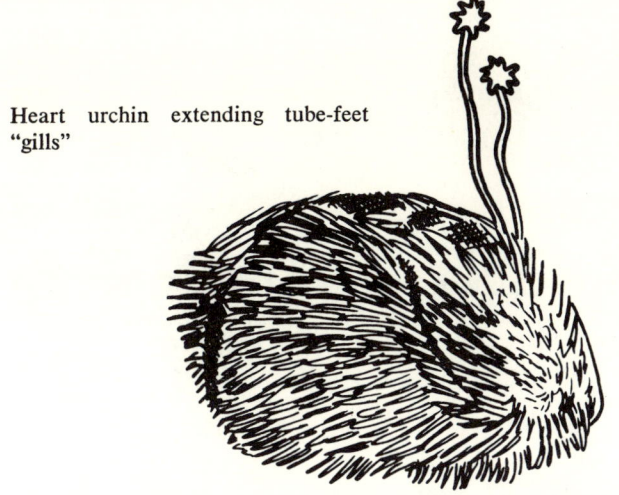

out of the water and pass it to the body fluids. The body fluids move it to every part of the sea urchin's body.

Food as well as water goes through the lantern, first into the oesophagus, then into the stomach, and the long intestine that coils like thick spaghetti on a fork around, and around again, under the test. By the time the food reaches the anus, which is a little hole up on top, it is nothing but waste. The nourishment is taken from it on the way and shipped like the oxygen all around the urchin's body.

There are five double rows of tube feet, running from the bottom close to the mouth, to the top. They sprout out of holes in the test seemingly by the hundreds, all of them thin-skinned. When the suction cups on the ends of the tube feet take hold of the rocks, it takes a six-pound pull to tear them loose. If an urchin is caught in the surf, he can rely on his tube feet to keep him from being

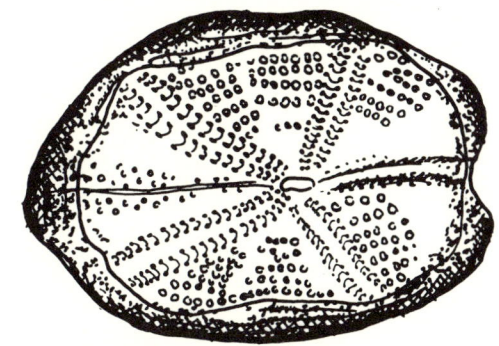

Test of heart urchin

Inside the test—a diagram

- tube feet
- spine
- ampulla
- water vessel
- test wall

Camouflage

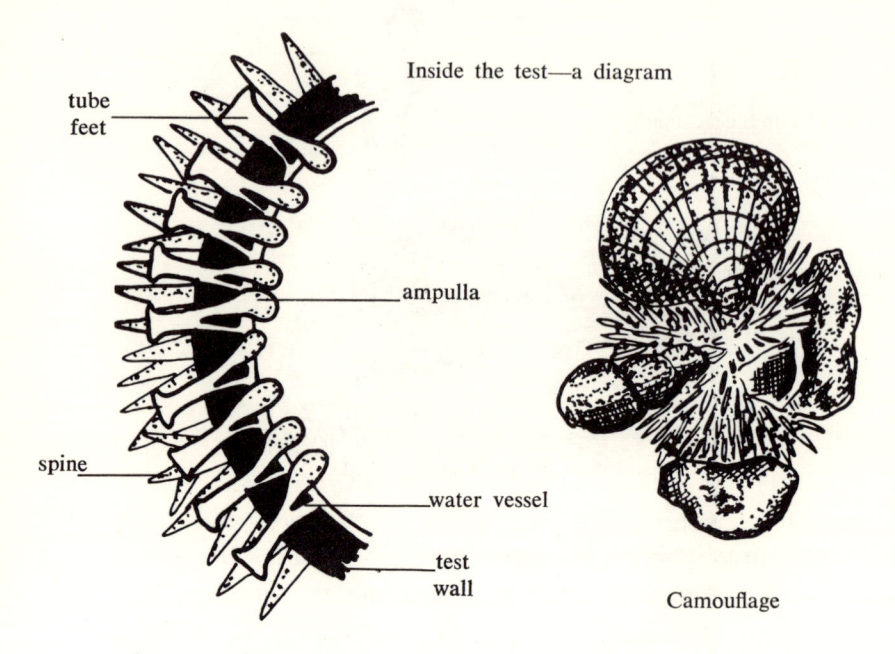

thrown about on the rocks. The heavy waves wash right over him and he remains in place. Tube feet are connected on the inside of the test to water-filled tubes. Each row of feet has its own water vessel. The vessel for each row swells out to hold extra water where a tube foot enters it, and narrows down in between the feet where there is no need for extra water. Each swelling is called an ampulla, and is muscular enough to squeeze the water within it out through the test into the tube foot connected to it. Filled with water the tube feet can stretch in every direction, and grasp by suction the objects with which they come in contact. Each ampulla receives signals from nerves when to fill and when to empty the tube foot connected to it. Some sea urchins use the tube feet to hold small shells and stones close to their bodies as a rough sort of camouflage.

Near the water vessels are nerves which send messages to the ampullae, warn the spines of danger, and inform the tube feet of food and "smells" in the water. There are also hollow tubes to carry body fluids from place to place. Some scientists claim to have observed the vessels contracting like blood vessels. Others say the body fluids are stirred by the movements of the animal, and that oxygen is spread from place to place by diffusion. This means that a large amount of oxygen or nourishment from food tends to spread out, until there is the same amount of oxygen and nourishment in every part of the body, and no concentration anywhere.

The thin skin of the sea urchin is covered with almost invisible pincers on stalks, minute hairs, and tiny cells which are called sense organs. These cells are connected to one another by a net of nerves, and the net hooks up to the larger nerves that lie next to the water vessels. There is a terminal tentacle located near the center on top. The sense organs inform the urchin of his world's events, for every urchin must know about tides and food, and the time to spawn. We would be unable to live with so few sense organs, but an urchin finds he has just enough to live very well among the rocks and waves.

No sea urchins ever even tried to take up life on land. They have remained dependent on the sea in every respect, including reproduction. They release eggs and sperm into the water when it is very cold. From March to May the eggs and sperm unite and form a larva which lives in the open ocean until it is ready to land on the rocks and change from a tiny two-sided, transparent creature into a round, spiny, cautious animal. It starts out very small and grows each year by an elaborate process.

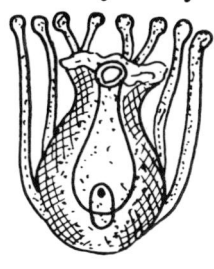

Larval urchin
magnified

Urchin stretching tube feet

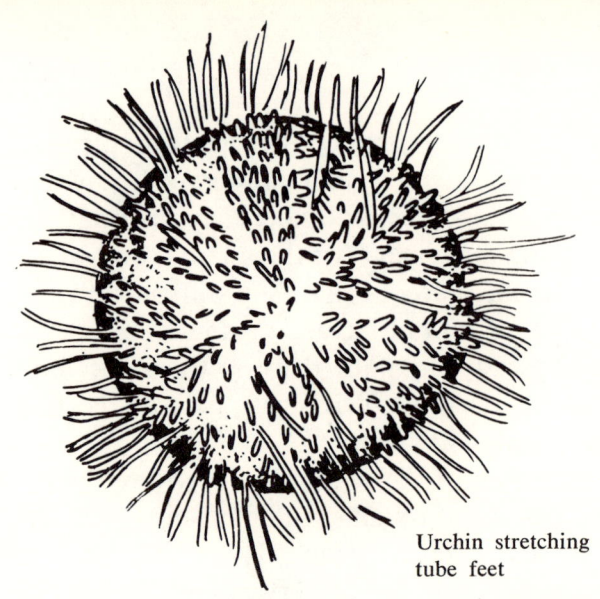

Since his test is not made all in one piece, like the shell of a snail, the sea urchin cannot enlarge it by expanding just one section. The test is made of many five-sided plates, and each one must be increased around the edge. Each year he secretes limestone around the edge of every plate. If the urchin made any of his plates much larger than the rest, his test would soon have a new shape. Later, after the urchin has spawned, brightly colored particles appear in his intestine. These are carried out to the white rims on the limestone plates and "painted" on them. The bright color sticks, and the following year the same growth process occurs again.

### VOCABULARY

arthropods — *very large group of animals without backbones, with jointed legs and body made of several different sections, or segments. Insects and crustaceans are arthropods*

camouflage — *a way of concealing or hiding by changing appearances*

concentration — *a large amount of a substance (in the case of an urchin, food or oxygen) in a small area*

terminal tentacle — *projection of thin skin with nerves sensitive to touch*

virulent poison — *a powerful poison*

Tidal pool

# HUNCHBACKS BY THE HUNDREDS CHAPTER 6

The small periwinkle

Slipping over the weedy rocks, trying to avoid the barnacles, we look down on the spiraled hunchbacks of hundreds of periwinkles. They roll when you step on them, making our explorations more hazardous, and they seem to be everywhere. Periwinkle is another name for a blackish round-shelled snail. Big and little ones are found along the ocean's edge all over the world.

The periwinkle has a spiral shell which starts with a small circle at one end, and turns around a couple of times to make a loop. Where the loop ends there is an opening. Head and foot come through this opening when the snail wants to move around and eat. When he wants to be protected from the air or sun, a wave or another animal, he pulls his head and foot back into the shell and closes it with a door called the operculum, which is fastened to his foot and rides along on top of it. The operculum is made of tough horny material, somewhat like our fingernails. The operculum fits the smooth, rounded entrance of the shell perfectly, and shields all the tender parts of the snail.

Usually a periwinkle does not stay on the surface of the rock waiting to be dried by the sun when the tide has dropped. A periwinkle searches out a crack, or a spot under weeds, or the hollow of an empty shell, and glues himself in place there until the water returns to cover him. Somehow the snail has a sense of timing about the tides, and gives himself time to hide. When he has found a protected spot, the periwinkle turns around so that the spiral of his shell points down. He secretes some mucus around the rim of the shell, and then draws himself completely in and closes the operculum. The mucus he left on the rim hardens in the meantime into a delicate skin that somehow generally holds him there, even though it often breaks and lets the winkle drop at a very slight touch.

Hanging delicately

The periwinkle has a long curled body which fits all the way back into the spiral of the shell. It fits perfectly because the shell is made in place. Certain cells in the infant snail are able to secrete a chemical which hardens as a shell. It is fashioned by a special layer of "skin" called the mantle, which clothes his body. Later the shell is enlarged by a special collar at a place where the neck would be, if a snail had a neck. As the periwinkle grows

A periwinkle out of its shell, a diagram

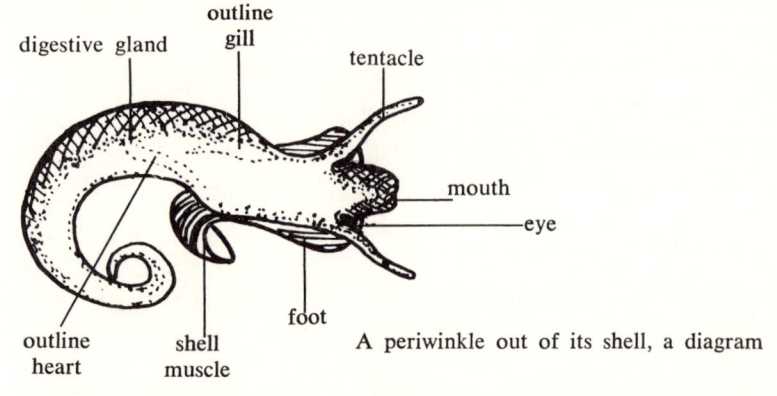

he can enlarge his shell around the rim. Periwinkles grow all their lives and some of them get as high as an inch and a half. No one has been able to find out just how long a periwinkle lives.

When the periwinkle comes out of his shell we can see two pairs of tentacles and a slit mouth. They sit on a head that is nothing more than a little knob. Behind the head, holding up the shell and also fastening it to the rock, is the foot. The foot is attached without a neck right to the head. And the body is on top just behind the head, concealed in the coiled shell. Head and foot are both modeled out of one piece. If you think about it, it is a rather strange union. A bit of foot slides along behind the shell holding up the trap door. The foot is very muscular, and tiny contractions in it move the snail along.

Up front on the periwinkle's head are the tentacles. One pair holds some simple eyes. These eyes don't see moving objects distinctly, but they are sensitive to changes in the light around them, and probably transmit simple danger signals. The other set of tentacles is used to feel the water, and plants and animals that might be in the way. They are peculiar tentacles, for they are hollow and can be drawn inside the periwinkle's head.

The mouth is nothing more than a slit, but it is not as simple and useless as it looks. Just inside is a tongue which is long and loosely coiled, with sharp teeth fastened in its surface. The teeth can't be seen without a microscope, but when the tongue is rolled out of the mouth over a seashore vegetable garden, the teeth scrape the minute plants off the rocks swiftly. They are so sharp and strong that they even get a little rock each time. Scientists have been able to measure in inches how much rock has been worn away by these sharp teeth over the years. The plants caught on the teeth are rolled back through the slit mouth, as if they were on a conveyor belt. All the periwinkles eat this way whether they live in the deep waters or high on the shore.

Periwinkles are the best examples we can find at the shore of animals who are giving up the sea and gaining the ability to live on land. We are suited to life on land and of course we don't even think about the special problems that a sea animal has to cope with if he is going to try to live here. A snail on land must resist drying in the air; he must also find a way to breathe with gills that were originally designed for under water. And he must be able to reproduce without depending on the sea to nurse his young through their infancy. Some snails have already made the adjustments. All the snails we know that live on land, or in fresh-water ponds, or in our aquariums, ages ago lived in the sea.

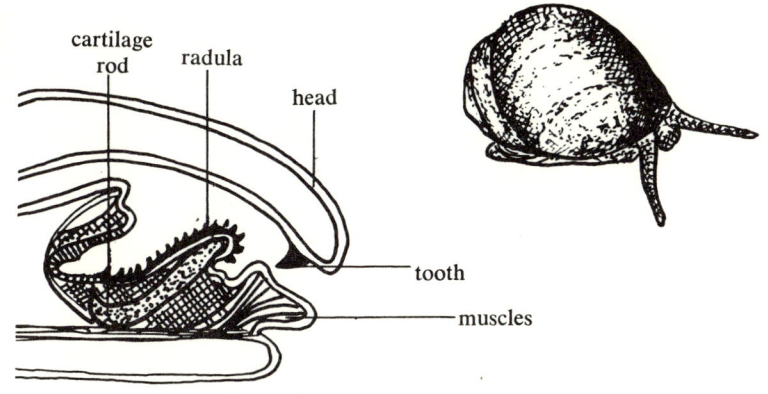

Enlargement of mouth portion

The rough periwinkle

High on the shore are two kinds of snails which can breathe air, and go for a long time without being wetted by the sea. These two types live so high on the shore that only the salt spray falls on them most of their lives. High tide comes there only every two weeks. One of them, called the small periwinkle, eats lichens and takes oxygen from the air. But for all its freedom from the sea it remains dependent on it for reproduction. From September to April, during the high spring tides, it sends fertile eggs in protective capsules into the sea. Living right alongside of the small periwinkle is another emancipated snail, called the rough periwinkle. It is a small snail that slips along on, and eats the microscopic plants that make the spray zone of the shore so dark and slippery. The rough periwinkle no longer depends on the sea for reproduction. The female snail protects its eggs in a cocoon inside itself, and when the baby snails leave the cocoon they are miniature, shelled adults, about the size of grains of sand. If the rough periwinkle lived among the waves, the infant snails would be lost in the sea at hatching. But high on the shore they can find protection in empty barnacle shells and other small places and escape being swept away into the sea. There are disadvantages you might not suspect

Shells of rough periwinkle

in giving up dependence on the sea. The rough periwinkle can't spread its young up and down the coastline as easily as a snail that lets the sea carry its young where it will.

The small periwinkle and the rough periwinkle could not live under water all the time even if they wanted to, because they no longer have a gill chamber designed to gather oxygen under water. In fact, if they are kept under water too long, they drown. In these snails the gill chamber contains a small gill and a much more important network of blood vessels which line the chamber and take oxygen directly out of the air. So instead of a water-filled gill chamber the splash zone snails have an air-filled one. They rely on the return of the water to their rocks every two weeks, not so that the gill chamber can fill up with water, but so the snail itself can keep from becoming too dried out.

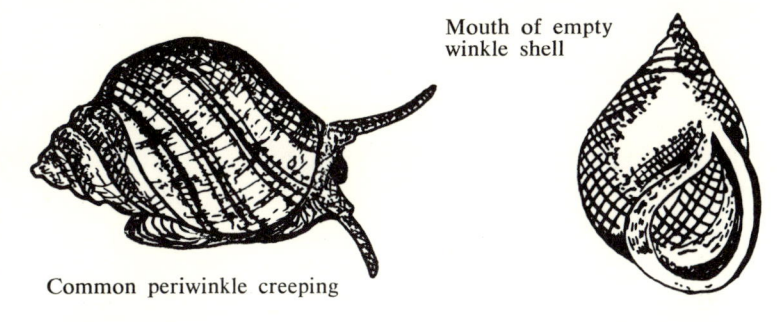

Mouth of empty winkle shell

Common periwinkle creeping

Most of the periwinkles on the rocks are common periwinkles. Despite the fact they live where they are lashed by the waves twice every twenty-four hours, there are more of these adaptable snails than any other kind. They can live on the rocks facing the waves, on sandy bottoms, in bays and even in the mouth of rivers, where the water is a good bit less salty. It is an unusual ability for a shore animal to be able to adjust to great changes in the saltiness of the water. For most of the sea creatures, changes that the common periwinkle can stand would be fatal;

their bodies depend so strongly on a certain concentration of salts in the water. But although the common periwinkle can adapt to many changes in its environment, it lives where it is covered at every high tide and depends on these high tides to carry away the little cocoons it makes to hold its eggs.

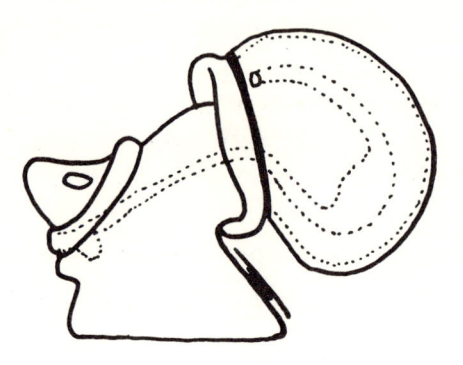

Diagram of larval snail

Periwinkles are either one sex or the other, and they pair up to fertilize the eggs produced by the female. Snails never learn to recognize the opposite sex by sight, or smell, so that after they gather together in large groups, they slowly climb up and down and around each other until by complete chance a male discovers that he is next to a female and can place his male cells inside the female snail with a little tube designed especially for this purpose. The female periwinkle coats the fertile eggs with a tough film which protects them when they are cast into the sea. The infant snails develop in the plankton until they are mature enough to seek the shore.

Far down the shore on the slippery weeds, so far down that it is hardly safe to look for them are periwinkles that cannot live in the air at all. They live under water or among dripping wet seaweeds. The flat periwinkle has developed a way to protect its infants, and doesn't spawn into the sea. It lays its eggs on a seaweed called Fucus, and later they hatch out complete little snails, only miniature. It is said they seek protection from the water inside a hollow place in the seaweed, and some of them, constantly hiding, can escape being washed out to sea when they are so tiny and lightweight. Once they have grown up a little bit, their lives are no longer so menaced by the sea.

VOCABULARY

simple eyes — *sensitive nerve cells that respond to changes in light by sending messages to the periwinkle's brain*

Limpets on a rock

# THE LUCKY INSTINCT

CHAPTER 7

The limpet is the only animal on the rocks with a home. It's true that a barnacle lives within a fortress, but who would call it a home when the barnacle cannot leave it freely and then return to it when he chooses. A barnacle's shell is more of a prison than a home, although he doesn't care a drop. A starfish is a wanderer, and a crab seeks out the nearest crevice as a hideout. A snail carries his house with him, camping out trailer fashion. But a limpet has a sense of where he's been and where he belongs. He returns at every low tide to the exact same spot. He gets there an hour or so before the tide goes out and he stays there until it returns. This spot is an oval groove on the rock where he feeds, and it fits the edge of his shell perfectly. If the rock is bumpy or the limpet's shell is irregular in shape, it doesn't matter. If the rock is soft, the limpet's shell wears away the rock; if the rock is hard, the limpet grinds down his own shell. However long he must grind, the end result is important. A close fit to the rock will mean life when the water drops at low tide. Air spaces under his shell could cause his death. A limpet does not worry about losing a little of his own shell. His shell is not sensitive, and wears away painlessly. It also can grow again. When a limpet fastens himself at his home he becomes a stonelike bump. He seems almost to be a part of the rock, for unless he is surprised he cannot be pulled off.

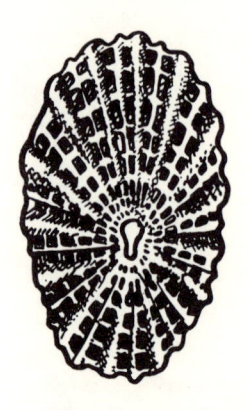

Keyhole limpet shells

The limpet has his own color. Yet sometimes it looks so very similar to the color of the rock that you might overlook him if there were not a shadow indicating the edge of his shell. A limpet can be almost any color, even pink, orange, or a lovely blue. But every limpet, no matter what his color, has a flat oval foot which holds him to the rock. No one knows why a limpet's foot has such adhesive strength. It can clutch the rock at the limpet's home, at the places where it feeds, and even when the animal is creeping over bits of pebbles where you can be sure suction alone wouldn't work. If you want to look at a limpet you must surprise him as he browses over the rocks, and with a swift kick or sharp blow knock him loose before he knows he is in danger. Once a limpet senses he is threatened he grips so firmly that you can no longer get even your fingernails under the shell. A limpet would rather be shattered to pieces than give up. The more it is teased the more tightly it sticks. Waves can't tear a limpet from the rocks because the shell is shaped so the water can't take hold of it. It is broad around the bottom, and comes to a small rounded cone on top. A common limpet is covered with smooth-edged grooves and ridges, and sometimes these stick out around the edge of the shell and make it uneven. Some limpets have smooth shells, and some have a keyhole in the top.

If you successfully surprise a limpet on his rock and turn him over in your hand, the most obvious thing you'll see will be a large cream-colored muscle. It is the foot. A limpet has one foot, without a leg above it. Its head is attached to the foot, and has a pair of tentacles and simple spots of eyes. The tentacles are useful for feeling the way and the eyes are sensitive to light. On the front of the head, a little way underneath, is a mouth. Inside there is a strong membraneous tongue, gently looped and fastened by both ends in a hollow inside the mouth. The tongue is called a radula, and tough curved teeth are fastened in it. The teeth are made by cells at the base of the hollow and as new teeth are formed the old ones move forward on the tongue. Near the cells which are able to form teeth, are other cells producing the membrane to hold them. The teeth and the loop of membrane rest on a lumpy mass of "cartilage," and muscles fastened to the mass push the radula out of the limpet's mouth when he wants to eat.

If the radula weren't so small it would feel like the surface of a rasp to our finger. As it is, the teeth can only be seen under a microscope. The long, hard teeth are used to scrape plants called algae off the rocks, and they wear down, just as a dog's claws get worn down from padding along on concrete sidewalks. The radula moves out and then it moves back. This happens over and over again, and soon a limpet has cleared an area of several inches around its home. Then somehow sensing the change of tide, the limpet starts to search out his niche. No one is quite sure whether he gets there by luck, a vague wandering search, or some kind of homing "instinct."

It is only fairly certain that a limpet heads home, and when he gets there he stays there until the return of the tide. Sometimes, if the rocks have stayed very wet he may go off to hunt more food. A limpet returns to his special groove in order to keep water under his shell each time the tide leaves him high on the dry rocks. Between his foot and shell there is a space where flaps of tissue hang. These frail flaps of skin must not dry out, for they are the gills. They are especially made to suit the limpet's

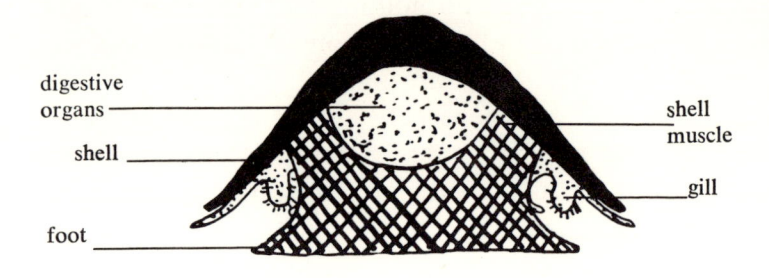

Under a limpet shell

special life. Under the shell, which is fastened so close to his home that no water can evaporate from inside, the gills continually take oxygen and pass it to the limpet's body. When the limpet begins to move around again tiny cilia draw in water and circulate it under the shell.

By looking at a limpet you can tell something about its life on the rocks. If the shell is high and the sides are steep, the limpet has spent a good bit of time defending himself against the rough seas by pulling his shell down tight against the rocks. To do this the limpet grasps the rock with his foot and tightens muscles attached to the rim of his shell. This lowers the shell over his foot and head and brings its edge into contact with the rock. If the shell is low the little limpet has lived quietly, perhaps in a tide pool, where its muscles have not been constantly

Low shell

High shell

pulling on the rim of the shell. When the muscles draw the shell snugly down on the rock they hold in the rim, and the shell grows tall instead of broad and relatively flat.

Limpets are unusual animals in another way. When they are young they are generally male. As they grow older many of the males change into females. Among the older limpets almost all are females. When the male and female limpets are mature, they send eggs and sperm into the sea to unite and develop into tiny swimming infants. The little ones float around, caring for themselves, until they are ready to seek the rocks, and their homes.

### VOCABULARY
adhesive strength — *the ability to stick to whatever is crept over*
niche — *crevice or crack particularly suitable to the animal (in this chapter the limpet) which inhabits it.*

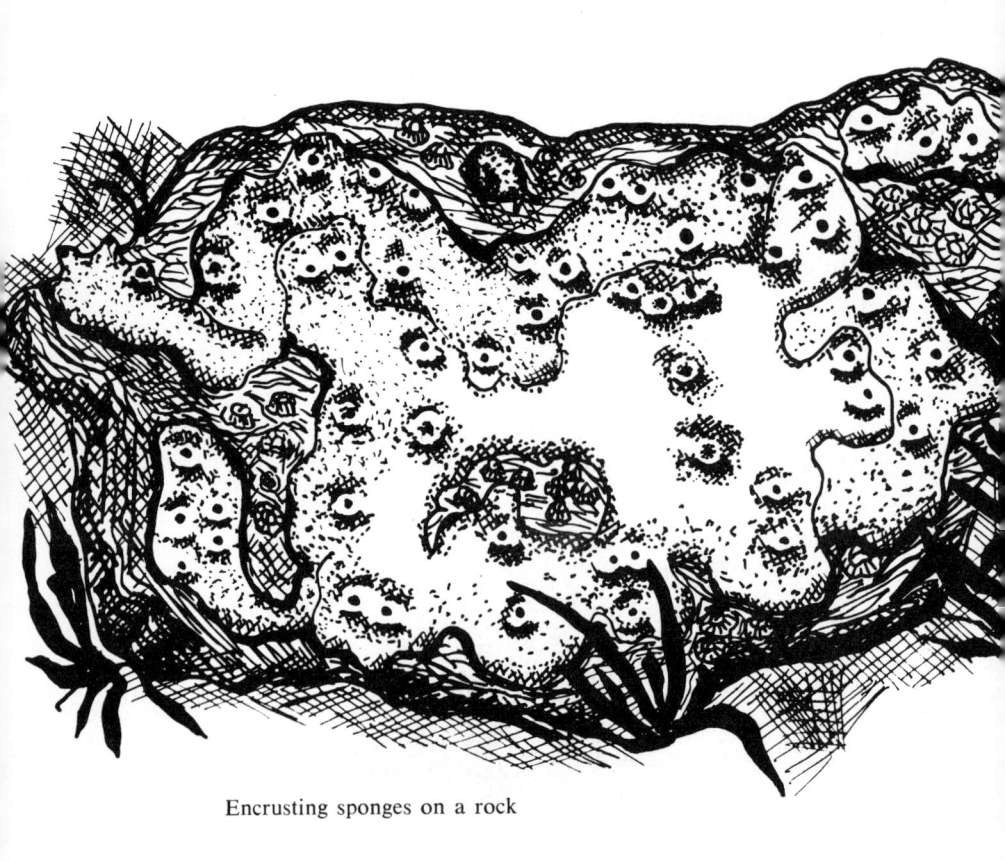

Encrusting sponges on a rock

# THE BUSY STRAINER

CHAPTER 8

What is animal-like about a mushy layer of vividly bright sponge coating the floor of a rock pool or encrusting the surface of a tide-swept rock? It is hard to imagine that a sponge is even a living thing, let alone an animal. But there it is, spreading itself thin in many places on the rock, adapting its simple living tissue to the beating surf. A common sponge can be very gay in color, orange or red, bright green, yellow or brown, but it is not a beautiful or symmetrical shape. We are used to huge bath sponges, from the deep warm seas, or plastic sponges which are only copies of the real thing, and it takes time to get used to sponges that lose their form, as pieces are broken away by the waves. Only in deep water, sheltered at the base of certain seaweeds, can a sponge grow a little taller and become a little more shapely. Also sometimes on the undersides of ledges you may find little vase-shaped sponges dangling in the dampness. But no matter which sponge it is you find, it still doesn't move at all, however long you watch it.

A sponge can easily be recognized by the little holes that speckle the surface. Or if you push it with your finger, you'll feel the thin layer expand again as the porous tissue fills with water. In this respect, a living sponge animal is the same as a bath or plastic sponge. Both of them have great numbers of internal cavities, and every space holds water. A sponge is a strange, simple creature. It

Right: Two kinds of spicules

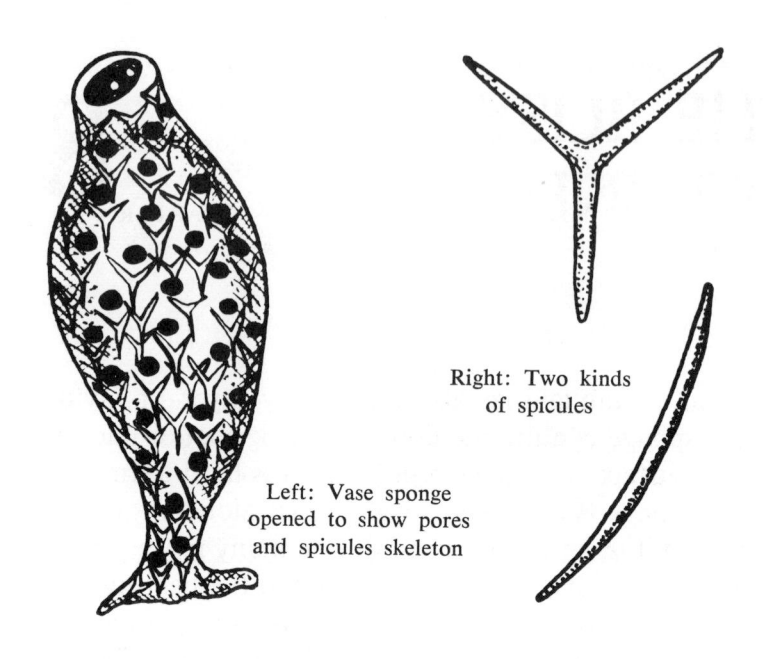

Left: Vase sponge opened to show pores and spicules skeleton

is made of just two layers of cells with a layer of jelly in between. It has no way to move about once it is fastened to the rocks. It has no nervous system or any other kind of system. There are no special groups of cells that work together as organs, so there is no heart, or stomach, no liver or brain. If it had nerves to communicate danger, there would be nowhere to send the message. Yet somehow, the cells that make a sponge always "remember" how to do it, and when buds of tissue are released, or eggs and gametes are formed and sent out to grow into new sponges, the cells from the parent carry the memory of just what the new sponge should look like. And they go about precisely forming the inside and outside, the jelly in between, the hole on top and the hollow in the center. Small hairs draw water through tunnel cells, and the sponge, with no "telephone" line from one spot to another, builds its skeleton neatly and starts to reproduce. All this is fairly amazing. But as nicely as sponge cells shape themselves into sponges, they have never developed organs or made any important changes in themselves outside of more complicated water channels. So that nothing ever developed from the sponges. No advances were made even on a simple level, as among the snails, where some members of the group changed enough to be able to live on land. Sponges are primitive, many-celled creatures, and they have never come to need any new abilities or organs to help them get along in the sea. They have lived exactly as they do today for millions of years.

The small piece of tissue that is released from the adult sponge shapes itself into a solid ball of little cells. It propels itself through the ocean waters by flapping microscopic hairs. Each cell has a single long hair which it waves as though it were on its own. When the infant sponge is ready it lands on a rock, or in a tidal pool, choosing a place that is always under water or very damp. There it begins to grow. The first thing that happens is that all the cells with swimming hairs move from the outside of the little ball of cells to the inside, and the cells that were on the inside move to the outside. Some of these make themselves into little tunnels from the outside to the inside. A hollow opens up in the center, and the ends of the tunnels open into this hollow. A large hole opens at the top. We see these holes, when the sponge has grown large, dotting the surface as it spreads over the rocks. The cells which moved in to line the inner hollow continue their rapid waving. These cells have long hairs

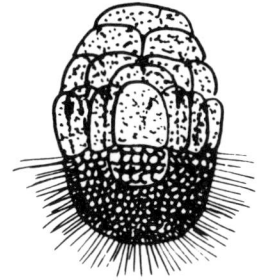

Sponge larva

Cells with swimming hairs move inside

or flagella that lash from within a special collar. So they are called collar cells. The waving hairs draw water from the ocean through the cells that turned themselves into tunnels. The water floods the central hollows and keeps them always full. The old water within is constantly being replaced by new water from the sea. Ocean water that looks so clear to us provides the sponge with all the minute organisms it needs as food.

These tiny organisms are not turned into liquid before they enter the body of the sponge, as they would be in the digestive systems of most other animals. Instead, the flagellated collar cells "swallow" the food up whole, providing it is small enough. They digest it and pass the nourishment taken from it to some wandering cells in the wall of the sponge. What cannot be digested, the collar cells "spit" out into the constant current of water that passes through the sponge.

Between the outside tunnel cells and the inside collar cells is a layer of jelly-like material. Traveling through the jelly are cells called amoeboid cells, which can move wherever they want. The amoeboid cells visit the collar cells for nourishment taken from the food. Then they travel around with it and feed the cells which can't feed themselves. The shape of the sponge becomes more complicated as it grows larger, and the location of the collar cells changes in the less simple sponges, but still the process of feeding is the same.

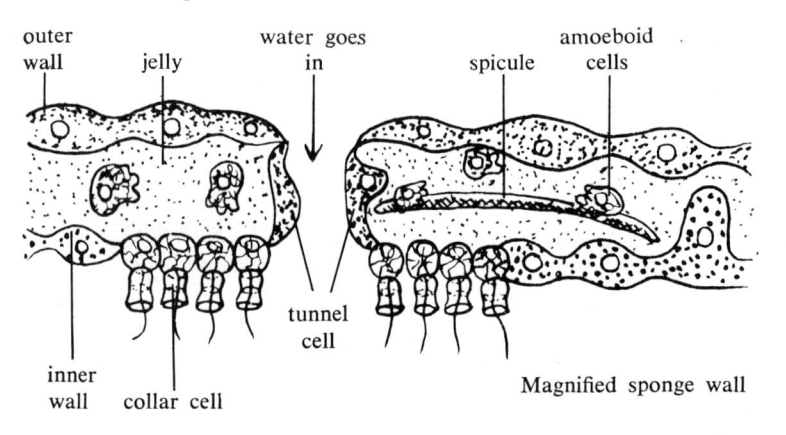

Magnified sponge wall

Small warm-water sponge

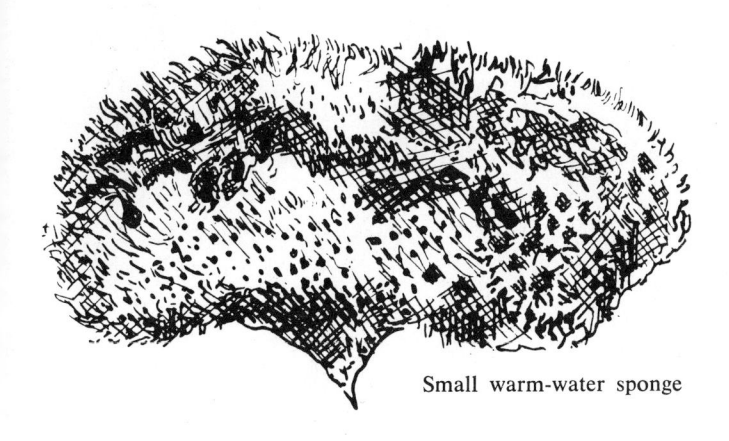

An amoeboid cell can change as if by magic into a collar cell or a covering cell. When some amoeboid cells enter the jelly, they divide into two, and drawing apart, they secrete a spicule. This is a hard needle, which has two or three points, depending on how many cells secrete it. These spicules are a kind of supporting skeleton for a sponge. Sometimes they are made of lime and sometimes silica. The sponge gets the mineral for its spicules from the sea water it drives through the holes in its body hour after hour. Some sponges add a horny substance called spongin to the spicule skeleton, and some support their cells and jelly with spongin alone. When we buy a true sponge, we are buying the skeleton of an animal that was once a busy sieve. Sometimes the warm tropical water held in all the spaces inside the soft, tough skeleton of the sponge houses hundreds of other little animals as well. But when we buy it all the small animals that used it for shelter and all the living tissues of the animal are gone. What we have is just a handy skeleton.

### VOCABULARY
silica — *a glassy mineral found in very small amounts in sea water, sponges take the mineral from the water to use for supporting spicules*
spongin — *the tough fibrous skeleton of some sponges*
symmetrical — *having a regular arrangement of parts*

Tidal pool

# THE FLOWER ANIMAL

CHAPTER 9

Softly waving in the gentle currents of water that stir around it, is an animal as beautiful as a blossom, the anemone. It is one of the most lovely creatures that you will ever see in the rock cracks and tidal pools. It is a rainbow animal that brightens up every dark and weedy space it lives in.

The anemone is beautiful, although sometimes it would be more truthful to say, the anemone has beautiful tentacles. Some of the Beadlet anemones have tube bodies that could hardly be more plain. The tubes of some of these anemones are nothing more than thick brown cylinders, sitting with one end snug against the rocks. Even though the skin is a soft and silken brown, the tube is drab and clumsy looking compared to the color and delicacy of the tentacles. But there are many other anemones that have tubes as radiantly colored as the tentacles on top, and some of them are decorated with marvelous patterns of stripes or dots.

The anemone does not have the most gracefully shaped body, but it certainly has a practical one. The tube is flexible and strong and can hold up all the tentacles without any effort. It can turn them in this direction and that, and most anemones can protect their tentacles from harm by swallowing them until the danger has passed. It's strange to say that this animal can swallow part of itself, but when the anemone is threatened by danger the tentacles surrounding the mouth are taken inside. But they are not chewed up and used as food. They are not digested. They are simply held out of harm's way for as long as is necessary. Although it seems that the tentacles are there to decorate the anemone for our pleasure, they are really there to gather food. And the tube body is not simply a stem to hold the "flower" on top. It is a place where food can be digested, a place where bits of food are turned into nourishment. Do you wonder what else the tube can do? It can move itself slowly from place to place on the rocks, and it can reproduce itself, or make the eggs or sperm to do so.

An anemone is a creature of mild habits, except perhaps when it is eating, or reproducing. It does everything quietly, and many things rather slowly and gently. The way it closes up is a good example. If the tube body is

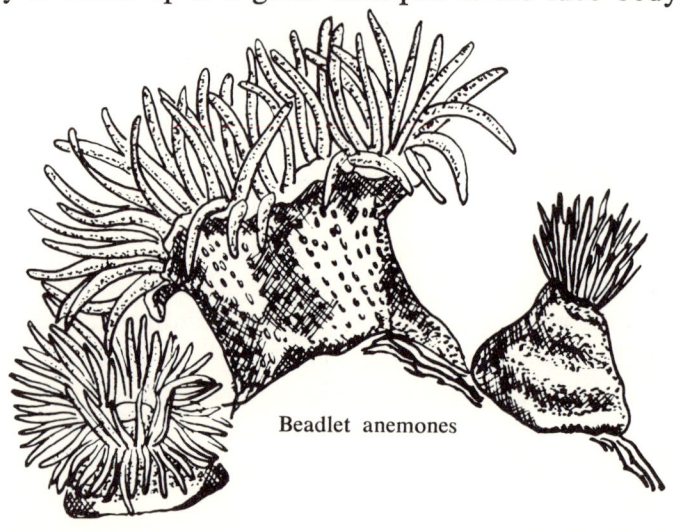

Beadlet anemones

Dahlia anemone

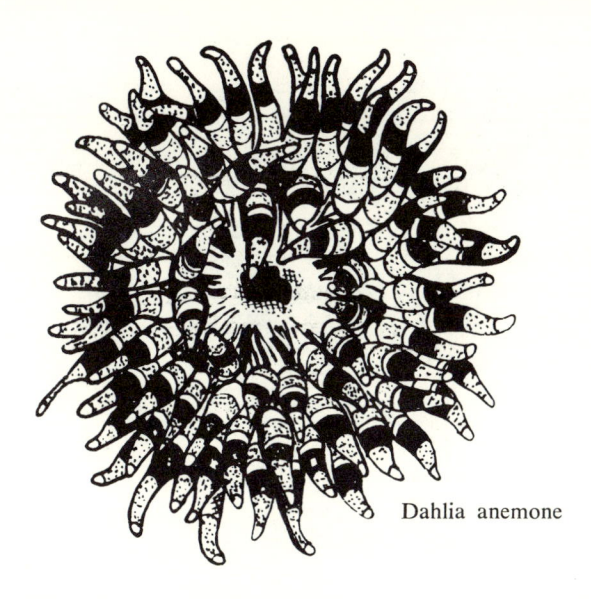

touched lightly, the anemone closes up within a few seconds. It makes no effort to get away, or actively to defend itself. It just changes from long to short, tucks in its tentacles, and becomes a quiet blob. It remains quite motionless until enough time has passed by for whatever disturbed it to go away. No other animals seem to like the taste of the anemone, but the flower animal does try to avoid getting torn or bumped, and that is why it closes. An anemone is slow to move from one place to another. You may be surprised to discover that an anemone has changed its location by several feet. How has it done it? By swimming away? By rolling? No, it hasn't rolled, even though it is barrel-shaped. The anemone creeps inch by inch over the surface of the rock, rippling the muscles in the base to move it ahead.

The tube is made of two layers, with a little jelly in between. Each layer has its own special variety of cell. A cell is a microscopic unit of a living animal. Each cell within an animal is made a certain way and can do certain things. Millions of cells, working with one another in big and little groups, make the tissues and organs of one

Inside an anemone, a diagram

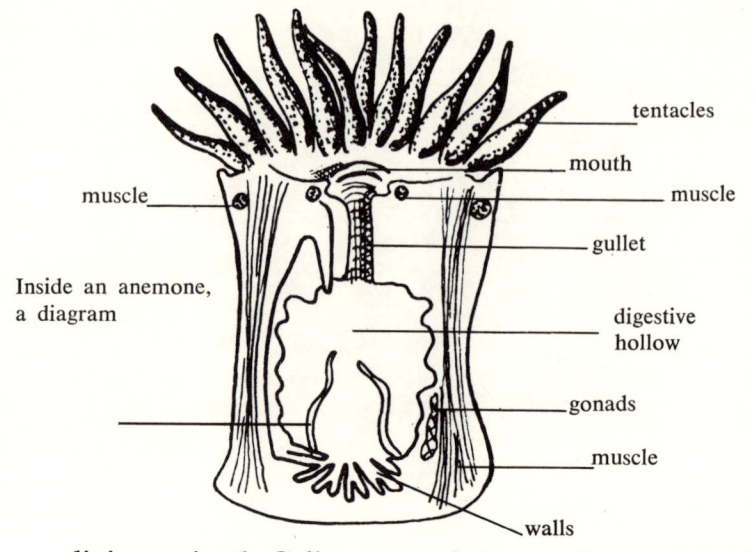

*labels: tentacles, mouth, muscle, muscle, gullet, digestive hollow, gonads, muscle, walls*

living animal. Cells are needed to make an animal, just as much as each brick is needed to make a building. Everything an animal does, eat and walk and grow, is done by the cells of its body. Cells on the inside of the anemone's tube secrete digestive juices that turn large bits of food into tiny particles. Other cells gobble up the particles and digest them within themselves. What an unusual way to eat! It's unusual because most animals absorb liquid food into the walls of the intestine, in much the same way that a blotter absorbs ink. But in the anemone the walls of the digestive cavity act like blotters that have suddenly developed mouths and a taste for fragments of crayon instead of for ink. They are able to *ingest* the food in the tube while it is still in very fine fragments. Cells covering the outside and cells lining the inside of the anemone's tube are able to make muscle fibers. The muscle fibers, pulling together, can change the anemone from a tube into a lump.

Since the anemone has no eyes or ears, it tells there are strangers around by tasting the water, by changes in the light, and by touch. In response to the falling tide, sense cells warn the anemone to contract to keep from drying out. An anemone cannot stay out of water, except for short periods of time in dripping, damp places. If it spent even five minutes in the sun, the animal would begin to shrivel up and in a short time more would almost disappear.

One of the most unusual cells in the anemone's two-layered body is the stinging cell that is complicated, and has a fancy name to suit it. Each stinging cell is called a nematocyst, and each contains as much poison as it can hold and a little dart. The tip of the dart sticks out of the cell a fraction, and the slightest touch sends it flying into

Stinging cells

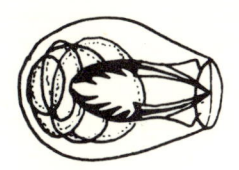

fired

Ready to spring

the object that disturbed it. The poison dart, and even the whole cell sometimes, goes straight into the enemy. Some of the nematocysts are on the inside of the anemone on long threads called lassos. Others are placed around the mouth, and most are on the tentacles. They all have the same use. The anemone stings all the tiny animals that bump its tentacles under water. Each animal that is stung is shoved into the anemone's mouth. If it still wiggles a little, it is stung some more at the inside opening of the mouth, and can be given a few last stings for good measure by the lassos in the digestive cavity. At last the poison works, and the tiny animal that was captured becomes food.

Some anemones have tentacles that look like masses of fluff. These animals capture the tiniest of living animals for food, by stunning them, in the way I have described, with the nematocysts. Anemones with fluffy tentacles eat such small food that it has to be prepared before it can be pushed into the throat. First it is made into a neat package with mucus, and bundled off to the tips of the fine tentacles. The tentacles then fold down to deposit the packages of food and mucus in the mouth. Inside the mouth are tiny hairs which move rapidly and sweep stale water and spilt crumbs of food out of the inside of the tube. But when food appears, the cilia change the direction of their sweeping motion and brush the food packages down inside. Everything works out so

Plumrose anemones

well, and the business of eating goes so smoothly, that you might think there is a brain somewhere. But nowhere within the anemone's body is there a brain-sized group of nerves.

The digestive cavity makes the food bite-sized for the cells of its walls, and for the cells that line the sides of the partitions. The partitions divide the tube up into many small sections, almost as though it is a room with too many walls. There are lots of cells to eat the food, for every side of every wall has cells to help. Inside the partitions, which are called mesenteries, eggs or sperm develop, depending on the sex of the anemone. A female Beadlet anemone keeps its eggs within its body. The eggs are fertilized there and stay inside until they have developed into complete, though tiny, new anemones ready for life on the rocks.

Many types of anemone do not produce their young alive. When the reproductive cells are ready they are heaved out into the sea in a peculiar way. The anemone empties its tube in the same sort of way that you could empty a tube of tooth paste by pinching it at the bottom and drawing your fingers toward the top, running them up from bottom to top until all the tooth paste squeezes out. The eggs or sperm don't leave the sea anemone at the first squeeze. They explode into the sea like white froth after several efforts. The eggs and sperm unite and develop into very tiny swimming animals that trail around the sea in the plankton until they are ready to take to the shore.

But anemones don't have to depend on eggs and sperm to make sure there are always new growing anemones on the shore. The tube body can reproduce itself in such amazing ways they seem like magic tricks. An anemone can creep over the rocks and leave little bits of the tube behind it as it goes. Each of the little bits can shape up and grow into an entirely new anemone that very soon becomes just as large as its parent. Or an anemone may stay where it is and simply draw on its base and leave little pieces of tissue around it on the rocks. These fragments can also grow into new, whole animals. In Japan there is an anemone that can throw down its tentacles one by one onto the rock where it sits. Each tentacle develops into a brand-new small anemone, and where the tentacle was thrown off around the mouth, a new tentacle grows to replace it. Another kind of anemone sprouts a complete band of tentacles around its middle. When they are finished, the two halves separate into two animals.

An anemone can do all these things with its tube, and it seems possible that it can do something else that no other animals can do. No one knows if an anemone ever grows old. If it doesn't grow old it can't die of old age. Of course, it can be killed by staying out of water and drying out, but if it does not die by accident, an anemone may live forever.

**VOCABULARY**
ingest — *take in for digestion*

Snake-locks anemone

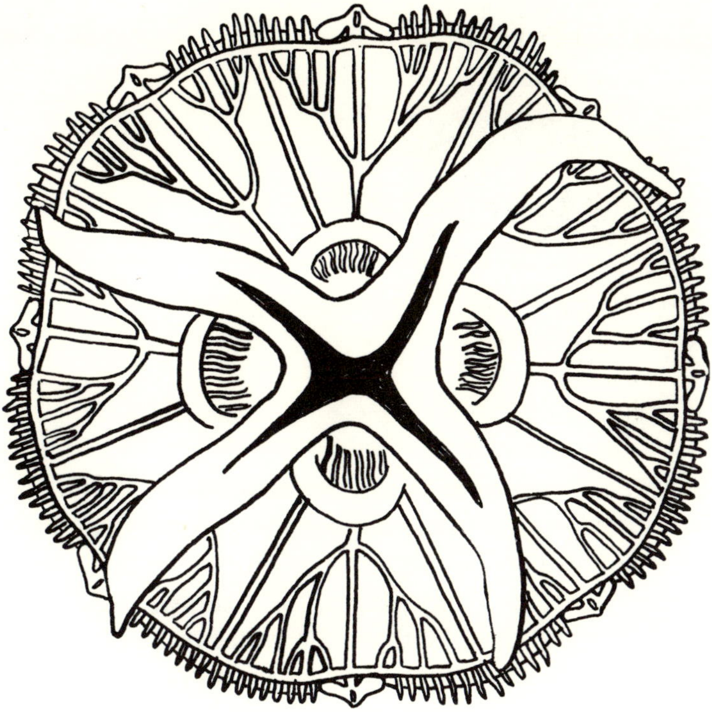

# FLOATING UMBRELLAS

CHAPTER

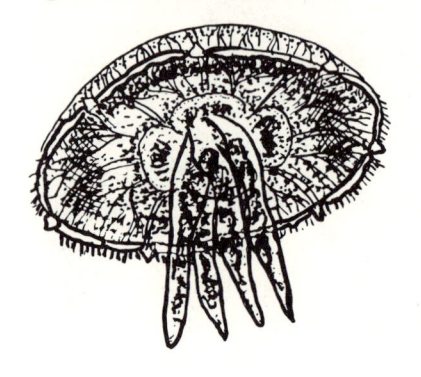

10

Late in the summer in the shallow water along the ocean's edge, you may find yourself swimming along next to a jellyfish. More often you will see it lying on the beach. There it is, motionless, for a shipwrecked jellyfish is injured and dies. Without the water to help support its mass of jelly it collapses, for a jellyfish is very weak and is unable to stay out of water, even for a short time. A jellyfish lying in a heap on the beach looks very little like an animal.

Under water a jellyfish looks slightly more animal like, pumping along in a leisurely fashion. Its body is smooth and umbrella or bell shaped. The bell is thick but it is flexible, and a jellyfish may stop momentarily and then go right on swimming when you touch it in the water, moving away with rhythmic jerks of its whole body. The jelly that gives the animal its size, lies between the two important, and very thin, layers of its body. All the layers of common jellyfish are colorless, and it's possible to look right into the inside of the animal. Sometimes you will see lavender loops floating there in the transparent body. Sometimes you will see reddish-brown stripes that look like decorations.

The most common kind of jellyfish is the Aurelia. It pumps along carrying its lavender loops and small tentacles that hang from the rim of the umbrella. The Aurelia's mouth is underneath, and the corners of it are drawn into four long flaps of tissue. The flaps capture small living animals and thrust the little creatures as food into the mouth. The animals that are sent inside are stung in the stomach and digestive pouches of the jellyfish by tiny cells that are very similar to the nematocysts of the sea anemone. The stomach and the four pouches break up the animals that are already small into even smaller fragments. The fragments are sent all over the body of the jellyfish in water currents that sweep through narrow canals. Starting at the digestive pouches the water goes out to the margin of the bell, then back to the center, and into the sea again through the mouth. The particles of food are carried along with the water and, on the way, many are taken into the cells lining the canals. They are digested right there within the cells, and everything that can't be used as nourishment is sent into the water canals again to be carried back to the ocean. The jellyfish nourishes its body while it swims along.

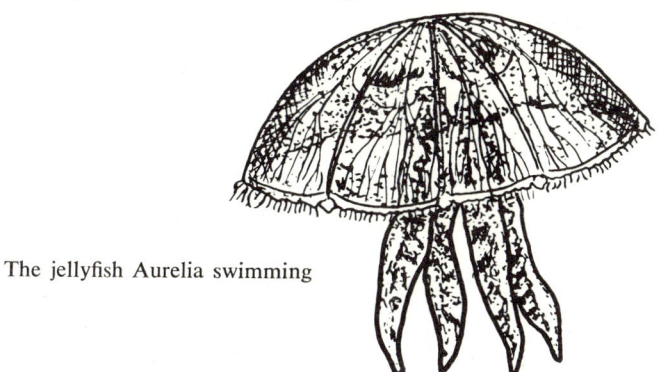

The jellyfish Aurelia swimming

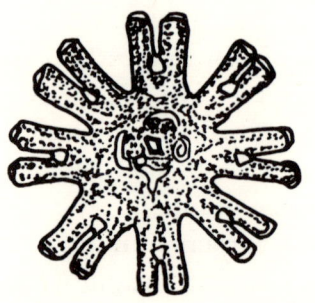

Ephyra larva

Around the rim of every jellyfish, whether it is young or old, are eight small indentations. Each one has a sensitive tentacle, a pigment spot that feels the light, and cells that can smell under water. A jellyfish could not control the pumping of its umbrella-shaped body without the eight indentations. An experiment once was done on a young jellyfish, that is called ephyra, to see how it regulates the rhythmic movements of the bell. One by one the sensory places were removed until only one remained. The jellyfish could still swim with one, but when that one too was taken from its body, it stopped swimming altogether, and lay motionless in the water.

All this time you may have been wondering about the four lavender loops that lie so colorfully inside the jellyfish. They are the gonads which are placed in the floor of the stomach so that water coming from outside passes over them. When the male jellyfish are ready they send their sperm into the sea where it floats around and finally is carried into the eggs of the female jellyfish by the water. The eggs are fertilized right inside the mother jellyfish, and the infants that develop from the eggs are called planula larvae. Soon you find that they have moved from the floor of the stomach to the flaps around their parent's mouth.

The larvae go everywhere that the mother Aurelia goes, until late in summer when she is swept by ocean currents toward the beaches and rocky shores. There the planula larvae leave the flaps around her mouth and search out places where they can attach and grow. Soon after the planula larvae leave their parent, the jellyfish begins to die. Often it is washed onto the beach, or falls apart in the surf or rough water just off shore. The infant animals never worry about the fate of their mother. They find places on the shore that are constantly under water and, once attached, they change shape, until they are long cones, each one fastened to the rocks by its pointed end. Over the winter each cone grows and changes some more until it looks like a stack of pancakes arranged from small to large. The edge of each pancake becomes eight arms, and sense organs develop. Now each pancake is an infant jellyfish. It is called an ephyra.

When the last changes have been made inside the ephyra and the last shaping of its body has been completed, the muscles running from one end of the cone to the other begin to contract violently. They jerk and pull so hard that they snap away from the outermost animal, and it swims off on its own into the sea. More contractions free the next ephyra from the stack, and it too swims away. Ephyra follows ephyra until all that were fully formed swim away to lead independent lives in the ocean. An ephyra is small when it leaves the rocks but it grows steadily and by the following summer, it is a mature jellyfish. It might be as large as 12 inches across.

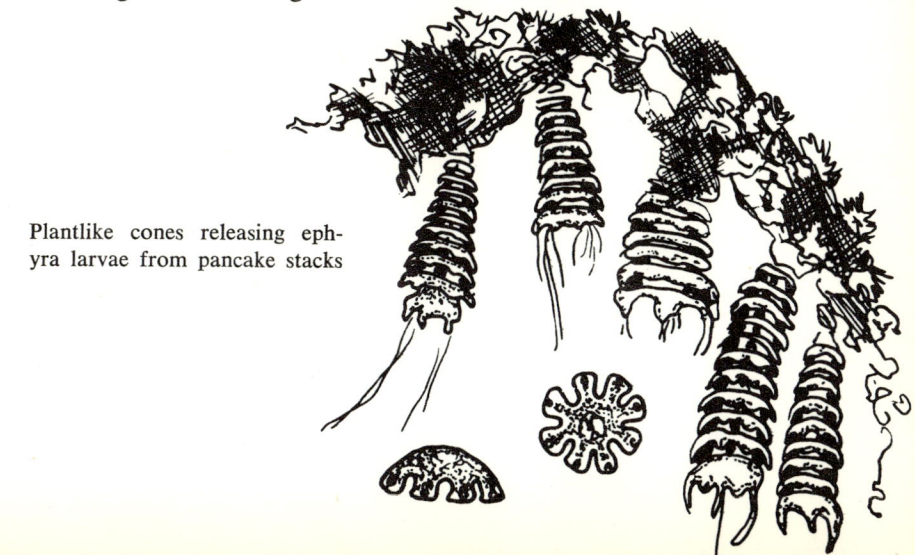

Plantlike cones releasing ephyra larvae from pancake stacks

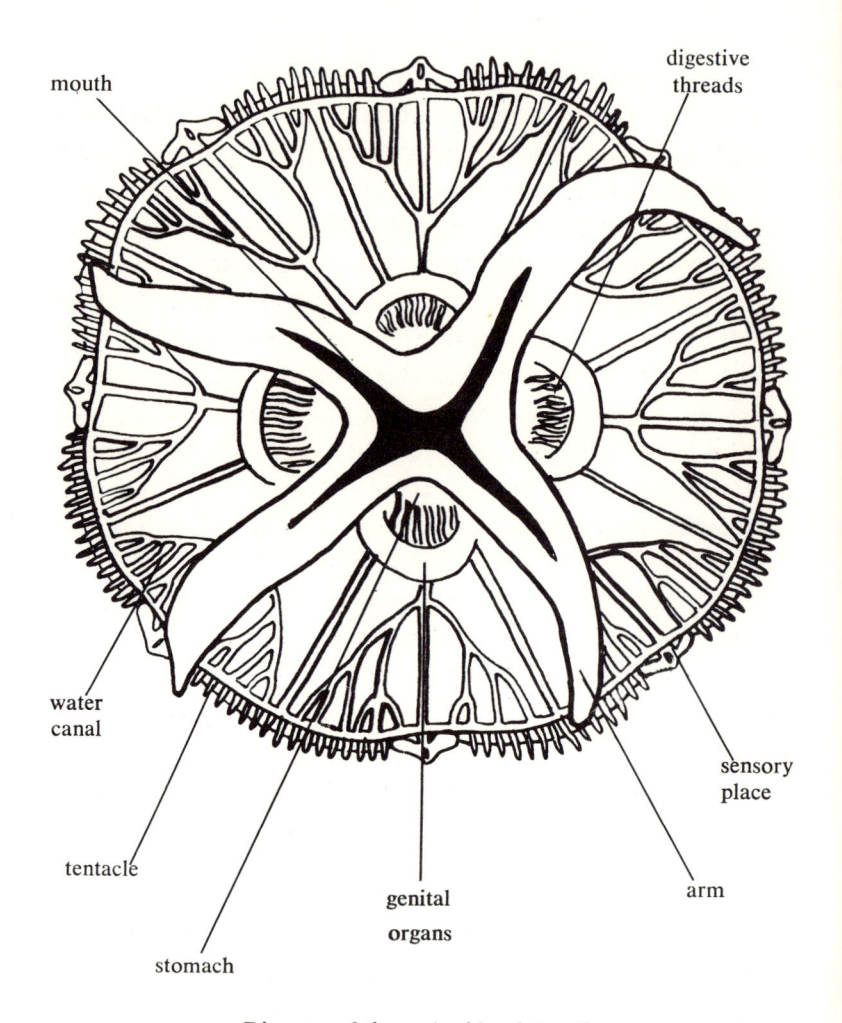

Diagram of the underside of Aurelia

Fastened to the rocks, the little cone that looks so much like a plant and so little like an animal, can duplicate itself by a process called budding. Just as with the anemone, a little piece of tissue shapes up and grows into a perfect little cone. You can be sure that there will be more jellyfish year after year whether or not the sea brings other planula larvae to the shore.

Many kinds of jellyfish float and swim with soft pulsations around the ocean. Some of them are very poisonous, with long tentacles trailing behind them in the sea. Often these long tentacles possess deadly stinging cells that kill almost all of the animals wandering into their snarls. And yet surprisingly, some small fish can adopt the poisonous masses of tentacles as a kind of foster parent, and live among them untouched by the stings. The tiny fish tantalize large fish into coming into disasterously close contact with the jellyfish, and its trailing, poisonous tangle. As the large creatures are digested the tiny fish catch scraps of food. It is hard to believe that many of these large jellyfish, just like the Aurelia, are summer creatures, with tiny plantlike winter generations.

#### VOCABULARY

digestive pouches — *in the stomach of the jellyfish, four sack-like sections connected to the rim of the bell by tubes or tiny canals*

alteration of generations — *some jellyfish develop from animals that are like tiny anemones. Such a process is called "alteration of generations."*

pulsations — *throbs or rhythmical beats*

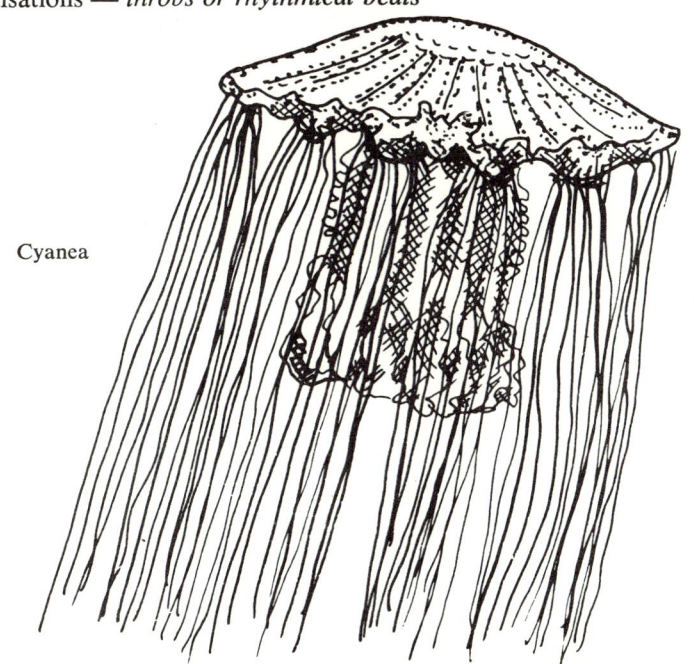

Cyanea

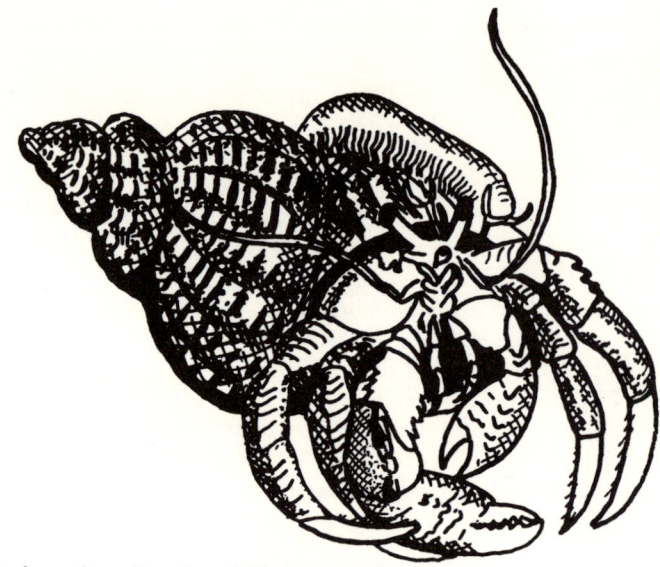

Facing a hermit crab and his worm companion

# A FRIENDLY HERMIT

CHAPTER 11

Rattling around on the shore, bumping over rocks, under and around the seaweed goes the hermit crab. If you take a closer look the little animal will duck back into his shell and hide himself behind his large claw, then tuck the other small claw in behind, and think he can't be seen at all. He is a pinkish orange and may be living in a nice dark brown shell, or maybe a black one, that long ago was deserted by the periwinkle that made it. Another kind of hermit will hide himself out in a larger kind of shell, very often a moon shell. Backed up inside, clamped in by his hind legs and closed in by his claws in front, the hermit can be rolled around the shore by the waves, and be just as well protected as was the snail who once lived in the shell. And if he is stranded by the tide as it deserts the shore, the small creature can remain shut in and not be dried out.

So here is a crab who does many things the way other crabs do them, but who no longer covers his back with a shell of his own, or hides in cracks under rocks for protection. You would know a hermit crab out of his shell

Hermit crab without shell

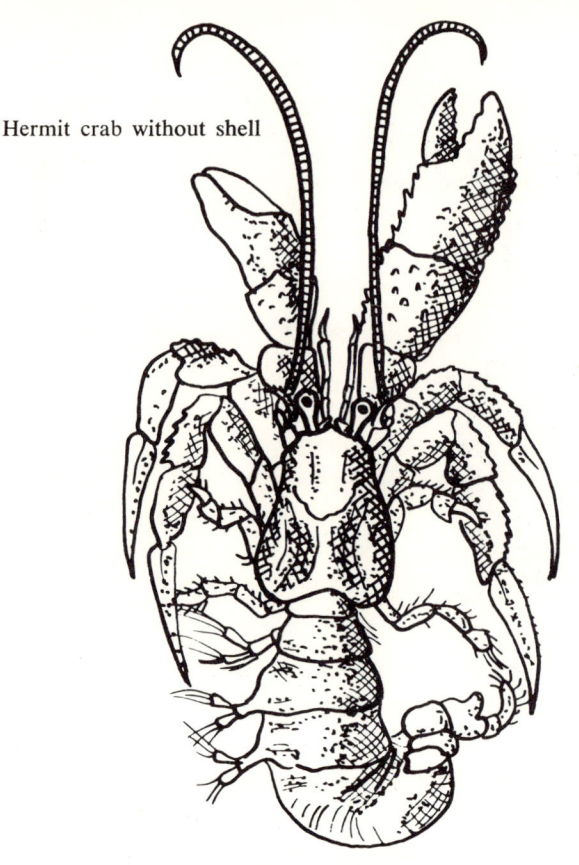

anywhere. The front part is shaped somewhat like that of a lobster, with two claws and two of the larger legs showing. But unlike crabs and lobsters, the hermit has a large soft abdominal section. This is the part which fits back into the snail shell, and clamps itself in with two hind legs. The two hind legs are both on the left side. The right side has lost its legs because they were never needed. As the years passed, the right legs became smaller and smaller and then finally disappeared. The abdomen of the hermit crab is not at all like the abdomen of the lobster. It is not a huge muscle used for swimming. Instead, as I said before, it is soft and holds some of the important organs of the crab. The liver is there, used in digesting food, and also the reproductive organs. A hermit crab would make good food for some of the other shore animals if he ever just walked out of his shell and remained unprotected. His abdomen would make easy eating. So he has to stay in his adopted home and take it with him wherever he goes.

The hermit is a scavenger like the other crabs living on the shore and will eat almost anything. Whether it is a plant or an animal, he grabs it in his claws and begins to tear it into pieces with the complicated limbs surrounding his mouth. The mouth parts pull the food into little bits and then stuff it inside the mouth, where it is chewed, squeezed, and sorted; then it is sent into the stomach and gut to be digested. Anything that is not digested passes through the anus that opens back of the abdomen. A hermit crab keeps a tidy house, and when he wants to pass some waste, he bends his abdomen down to the opening of the shell house and leaves the waste outside.

When the hermit crab grows too large for the exoskeleton covering most of his body, he molts in order to grow larger. He hides deep in the snail shell to molt, and sheds the covering on his abdomen first. After that, he molts the shell covering the portion of his body sticking out of the shell and then the coating on his eyes, his legs, and claws. Soon he grows too large for his shell house and must look for a bigger one. Off he goes, clattering over the rock with the old snail shell on his back. The hermit crab cautiously examines every new shell that looks as though it might be large enough to make a fine house. First he turns it around and around, and then he peers into it and feels its innermost crannies with his claws. When he is sure no one else is living in the new shell, and that no enemy is ready to snatch him up from the water around, he prods and pokes it a few more times with his antennae and then cautiously he starts out of his old house. He retreats a few times, as if he can't make up his mind, and then suddenly he makes the change, backs into the larger shell and clamps himself in. Once he is in he is fastened so firmly that you can get him out only by breaking his body, or the snail shell. A hermit crab can let himself out of the shell, and when it seems safe, he will emerge a little, feel around with his antennae, and start out to look for food, dragging his shell behind him.

The lucky hermit, who is not a hermit at all (for a true hermit is supposed to live all alone) is the hermit crab who lives with a sea anemone on top of his shell. With an anemone for a companion he never needs to find a larger shell. The anemone wraps itself around the shell and its body grows together underneath. It drapes the opening of the shell as a kind of front porch. The anemone scavenges the crumbs that fall to the rocks as the hermit crab rips up his dinner.

Very often a little ragworm lives inside the hermit's house, working as a kind of chambermaid—sweeping out the dirt and crumbs from dinner, moving the stale water around, and freshening it. Just like the anemone, it picks up scraps that are left from the hermit's dinner. When two animals live together this way, making life better for both of them, it's called commensalism.

In reproducing, the eggs are carried by the female hermit on the small dwarf legs of the abdomen. The eggs develop inside the shell house until the larvae are ready to be released into the ocean plankton. Often while the eggs are growing, the female hermit pulls far out of her shell, looking first to see if the coast is clear, and waves them around in the clear water. The little developing eggs must have oxygen, or they cannot grow. When at last they are ready the microscopic larvae hatch from the eggs and swim off into the sea to live independently. They stay in the plankton until they are ready to locate tiny snail shells, and take up life as hermits.

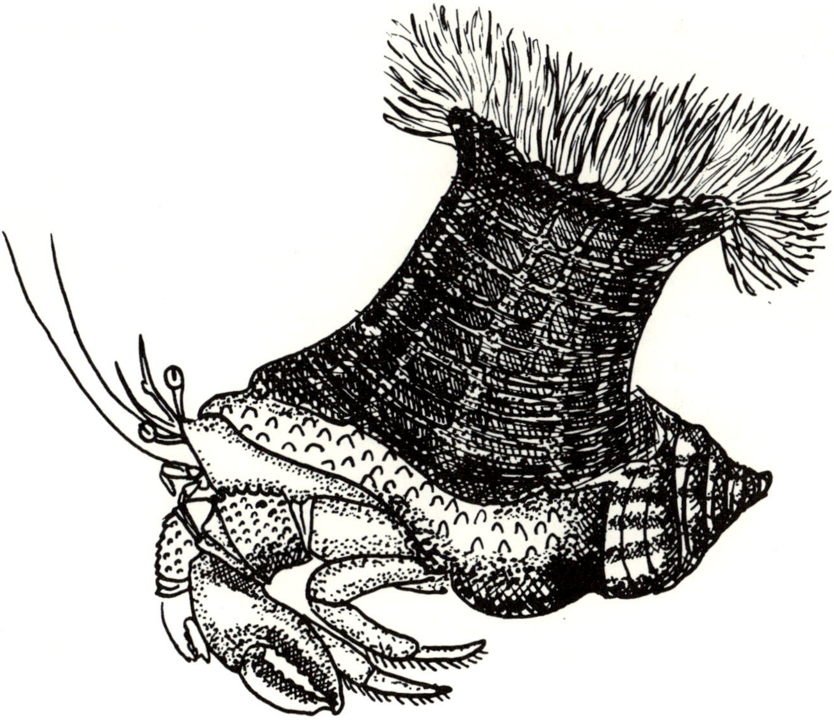

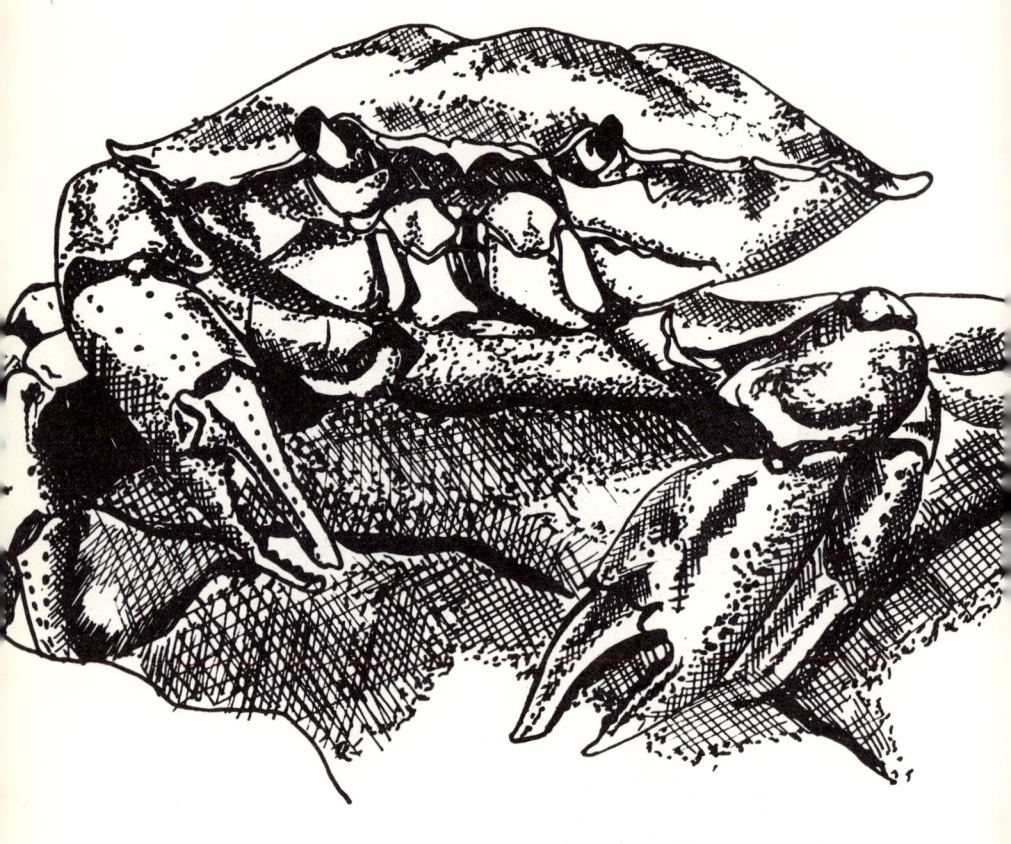

The angry crab

# THE CAUTIOUS CRAB

## CHAPTER 12

If you bend down to look deep into a dark crack, if you move some tangled seaweed, you may suddenly find yourself staring into a pair of beady, black eyes on short stalks. The eyes belong to a crab, one of many that lurk in hiding places all over the shore. Some crabs, especially of the kind called Carcinus maenas, live in extra salty pools, evaporating in the sun high on the shore. Other carcinides live in pools made partly fresh by streams flowing by them into the sea. From high on the shore to the deep water, carcinides lurks ready to fight, pincers poised to seize anything edible that comes his way. He has been nicknamed by the French, le crabe enragé, the angry crab. Just let a small fish, a long worm, your finger, or almost any living thing approach him, and carcinides lunges with open claws. He may be a large crab; he may be small; he may be dark, black-green or somewhat red; but whatever his size and color, he is savage and eager.

In summer, Carcinus lives on the shore but in the winter when the cold air on land makes the tidal waters too cold, he retreats down into the deeper ocean waters, which strangely enough are warmer than those on the shore. A crab is cold-blooded, and the colder the sea water becomes, the more his body temperature drops. A crab doesn't mind being as cold as the winter sea, where the deep water is just warm enough to keep his flesh from freezing and let him move around to eat. But he must

Crab larvae

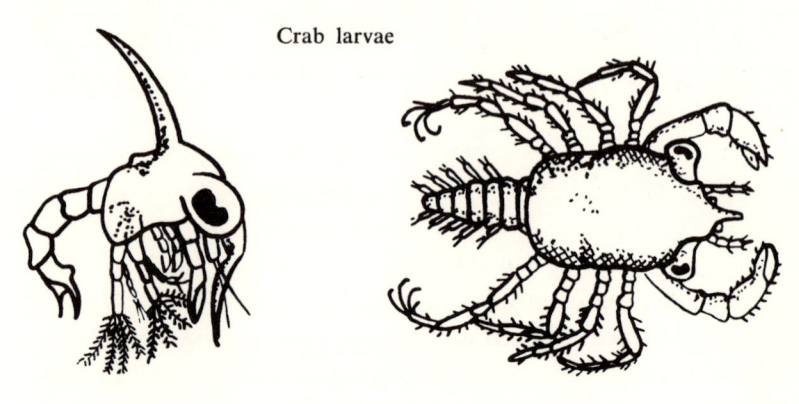

avoid the shore, where the air can almost freeze the salty tidal pools, and the crab would become so sluggish he would starve. While a crab is offshore in deep water, the males and females spawn, and the eggs that are formed become larvae that live in the plankton. The larvae change form as they float, several times as infants, and then a few times more as they develop adult features. The small young crabs live in the rock cracks, leaving them, when they become older and wiser, for the deepest waters of the tidal zone, where the ribbon-weed Laminaria grows.

A crab carries its skeleton on the outside of its body. The part that covers the largest portion is called the carapace. It is easy to recognize, for it is broad and fairly flat and has eyes at the front, where the head section is, and claws and legs at the sides, and a tucked-under flap of an abdomen at the rear. Under the shell with its tiny lumps and knobs are all the important internal organs. There are all the things that you might expect—a mouth, stomach, gut, reproductive organs and gills, and perhaps unexpectedly, there is a heart. Of course a crab's heart does nothing for his temperament. It's only there to pump blood and oxygen around his body. The gills are the oxygen gatherers, and they are all in a couple of small spaces, especially designed with holes to let the sea water in and out. The gills are thin, almost like sheets of paper in a stack. The ocean water seeps between the sheets and leaves oxygen as it passes.

A crab's legs all attach beneath the broad carapace. The first pair are claws. They will give you a proper welcome if you are not careful when you explore. The pincers are strong and the crab is fast. The four pairs of legs behind the claws tell us a lot about the lives of different crabs. If they are pointed it means the crab is a walker and uses the points of his legs to give him a grip on the sides of the rocks. Crabs with very sharp points can fasten themselves so flat against the rocks that the pounding surf can't move them at all. Broad paddles on the long jointed legs tell us that a crab travels by swimming. The hind legs have other uses too. One kind of crab uses the very back pair to hold seaweed over him for camouflage, while another hides beneath pieces of sponge which grow into place and make him look like a crusty rock. But a crab is a crab, and though he uses his pincers for frontal attack, when he is attacked himself he darts off sideways.

A crab's legs are long and jointed. Outside they are hard, and where the sections meet there are leathery joints. Inside, connecting the sections, are soft, strong

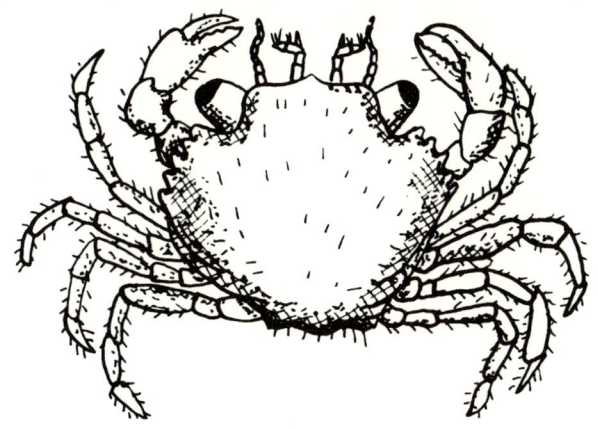

Infant shore crab

muscles. The muscles, which open and close the claws and that move the legs and greedy mouth, are all attached inside the skeleton. Crab blood flows through vessels in the legs, supplying the muscles with food and oxygen. Messages are carried to each muscle in each leg to tell it how to behave. And when a crab gets a leg caught be-

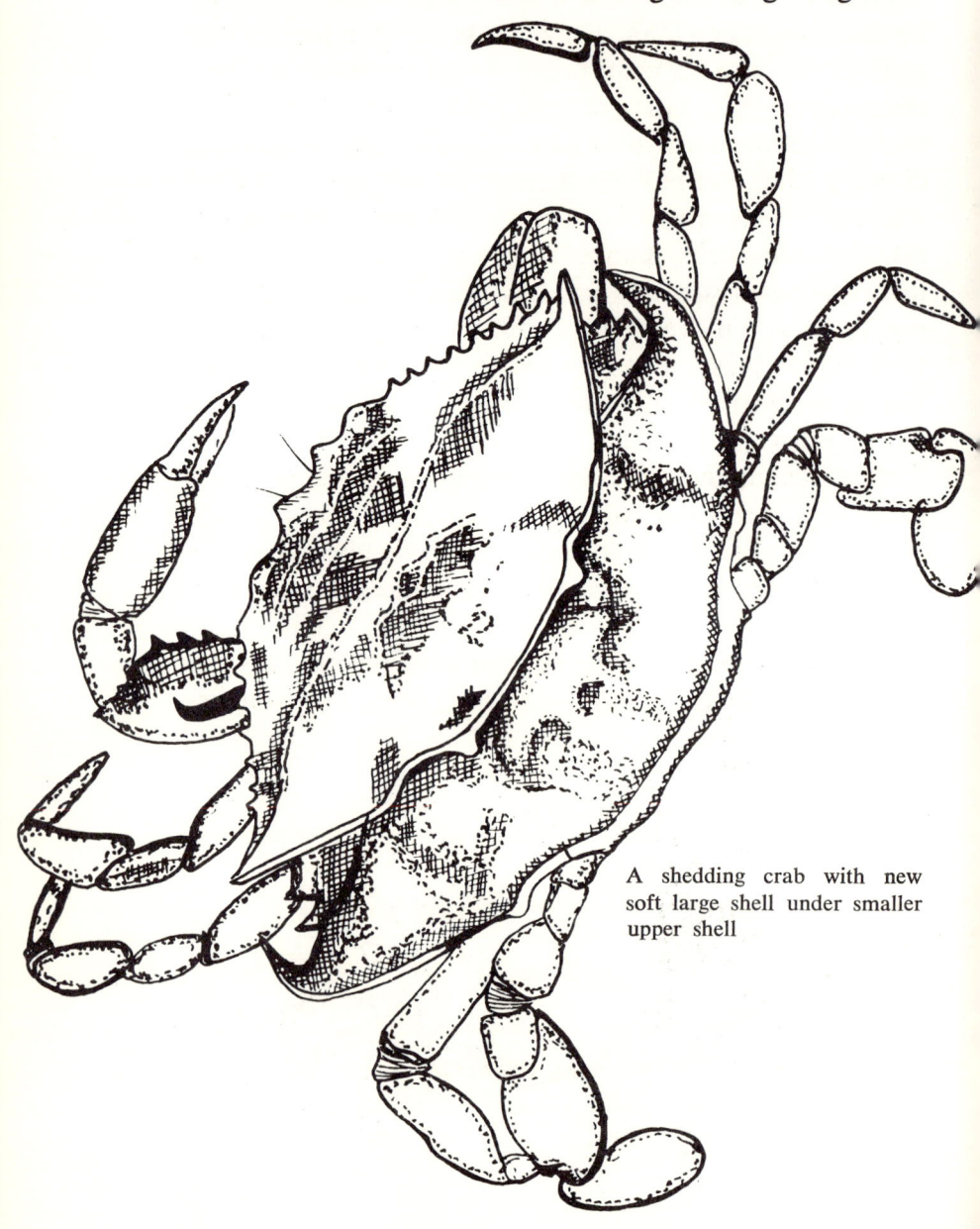

A shedding crab with new soft large shell under smaller upper shell

neath a tide-tossed stone, his nerves carry a very special message to certain muscles in the third joint of the trapped leg where there is a deep groove. The message that comes when the leg has been caught, tells the muscles to pull and twist until the groove splits open and the leg breaks off. The crab doesn't plan to break his own leg. He has no choice. His muscles get the message and he walks away without his leg. But for all the inconvenience of having to leave part of himself behind this way, a crab often saves his own life. The wounded leg heals over, drawing the exposed nerves and blood vessels inside. Who could say whether the crab has felt pain? At any rate, in a matter of months a new leg replaces the one that was lost. The lost leg or claw is replaced by molting, which is the way a crab gets a new shell of a larger size. Each time a crab molts, the new leg grows larger and begins to look exactly like the old one. This is called regeneration.

When the crab steps out of his split carapace, he is naked and uncertain. His new shell is still a limp skin on his soft, growing body, and it will be several days before it is hard, so the crab who was a seashore "terror" a few hours earlier is now defenseless. And what a tasty meal he makes for his enemies, unless he hides himself deep in the rocks until the slow hardening process is finished.

### VOCABULARY
fresh water — *water that, unlike the ocean, does not have a large amount of salt*

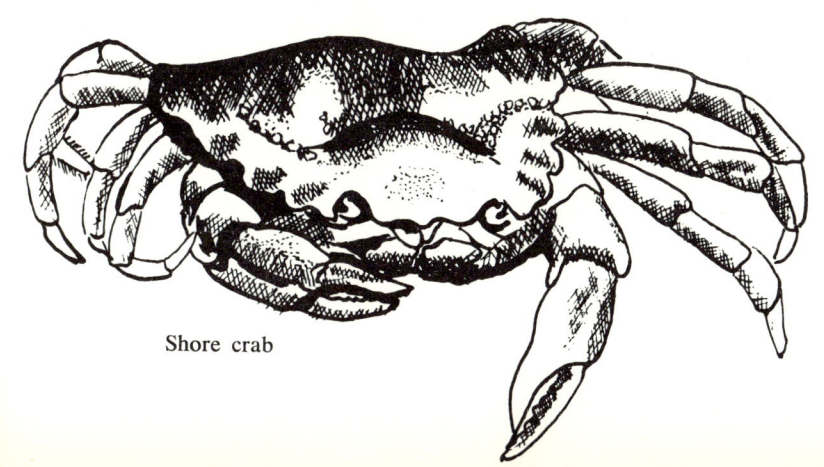

Shore crab

# HIDE AND SEEK

CHAPTER 13

Mole crabs fishing

Have you ever lain on the sand in the shallow wash of water left by the last curling wave? When a wave breaks, it runs up the shore thinning out until it is only a few inches deep. Some of the water runs back to join the next breaker. Some of it sinks into the sand. If you have flopped, stomach down, and dug in your toes, feeling the waves come and go, you have probably also had the notion that someone was tickling your feet as they curled beneath the sand. And you may have noticed little round holes, that send up a few bubbles when the water washes in again. Don't be alarmed if I tell you that the someone tickling your feet was a tiny crab. Well, it was, but not a biting crab. It is a digging crab that lives on the sandy shore.

It is not easy to live on sand. The water rushing across the surface grabs everything that is there, moving the top layers of sand, the small stones and the deserted shells. It turns them over, twists them round, picks them up and throws them down again. Things that are light enough are rolled under the waves and carried out to sea, or thrown high on the beach. A small animal might lose some legs among the tossing pebbles, or be dragged to deeper water where it could not feed. Or it might be thrown into the air and scorching sun. All these things would happen to the mole crab, if the mole crab could not dig itself into the sand and avoid the strongest rush of water. It has legs that are designed for rapid digging. Just try and catch one. You will be amazed at the pile of sand you turn up before you find the crab. These little animals move up the shore in the surf until the tide is at its peak. As the tide retreats so do they, until the tide has dropped to its lowest point. They always stay where the water is shallow and they emerge for a second or two each time it recedes, sweeping through it with their feathery antennae. They don't come all the way out of the sand, but just far enough for their antennae to comb microscopic organisms out of the water. The hairs on the antennae are so fine that they can even catch bacteria. When mole crabs have some food on their antennae, they stop combing and run them through their mouth parts to clean them off. By this time the water is disappearing, and so are the mole crabs. They wait under the sand for the next wave. Mole crabs don't see much, indeed their food is so small that it cannot be seen and captured. It is merely netted and eaten. Mole crabs don't exactly socialize with one another, but they do act in groups. When one crab raises its nets all the other crabs nearby do the same thing. They all move up the beach, and they all move down the beach. Sometimes one mole crab is left behind by its fellows moving downshore with the tide. Then, having no way to get down to the water's edge without being seen, the lone crab digs down into the wet sand to wait until the tide comes in again.

You might wonder who would see a mole crab if he came to the surface of the sand and scampered down to the water's edge on top. It seems as though no one could be watching the sand that closely. But the beach always has birds inspecting it for food. Some fly high above it looking for fish in the shallow water. Many hop along the water's edge looking for a delicious mole crab to eat. And so when a mole crab is stranded high on the shore he digs in and waits. Under the foaming edges of the waves at high tide, he can join the other mole crabs and safely retreat down the beach. Other dangers lurk where the water grows deep enough for fish. If mole crabs go too deep into the sea they are likely to be eaten by fish who are constantly poking and prodding the sand, looking for their pinkish, tan bodies. A mole crab wouldn't like to admit it but he is an important source of food for birds and fish. Since these animals have no way to gather microscopic plants and animals directly from the sea, they get them indirectly by eating the mole crabs who collect and thrive on the floating particles. Mole crabs can turn the nourishment taken from millions of microscopic animals into flesh. If the sea is rich with food, there

Full side view

Top view

will probably be lots of mole crabs. Many mole crabs can keep many birds and fish alive. For no matter how rich the sea is in plankton and microscopic animals, the larger animals would starve without the mole crabs to play fishermen.

A mole crab has a short life. He doesn't live as long as a lobster and nowhere near as long as the ageless anemone. A mole crab lives only two summers and the winter in between. The first summer is spent growing, changing from the tiny, transparent larva that left the orange egg on its mother's abdomen, into a creature recognizable as a mole crab. While it is a larva it drifts far out over very deep ocean waters, then it floats back to shore with the currents, and starts living on the moving sands of a beach somewhere. It eats and grows, moving up and down the beach with the tides until winter comes and it seeks deeper, slightly warmer waters. It keeps right on growing all winter, and by spring is mature enough to reproduce. Mating is the important event all the crabs have been prepared for, and after the eggs of the female mole crab are fertilized most of the male crabs die. Life is over for most male mole crabs by July. The mother crab carries her bright orange eggs up and down the beach with her until the eggs are ready to hatch. Then near hatching time she stays in deeper water to make sure none of her infants are lost on dry sand, when they come from the eggs. The larval mole crabs join the plankton and the same story could be told about their lives, over and over again, generation after generation.

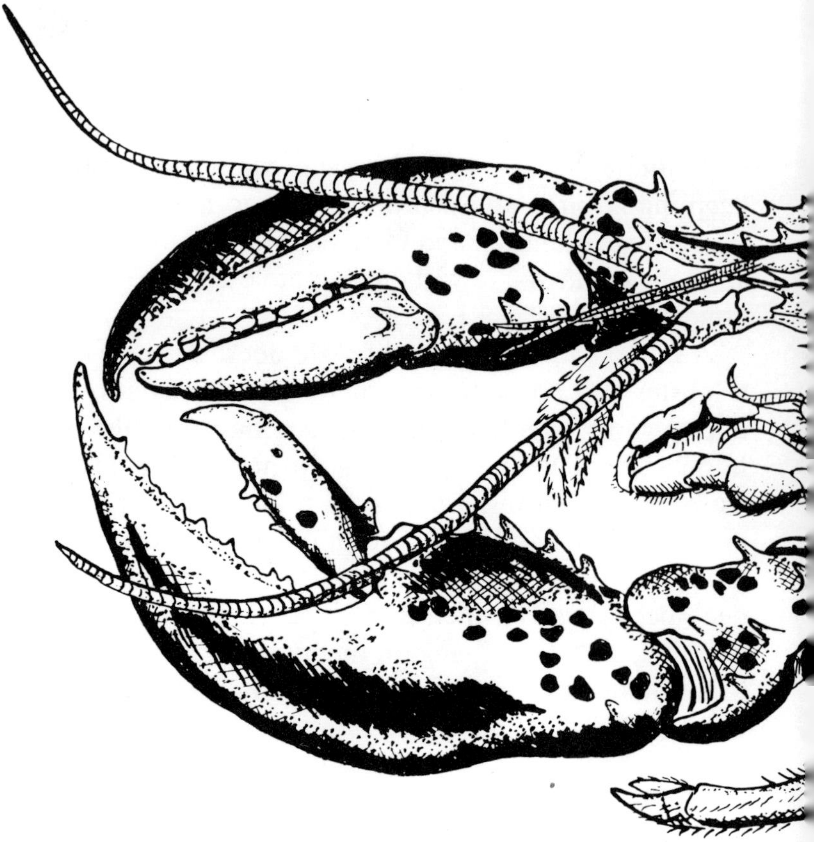

Maine lobster

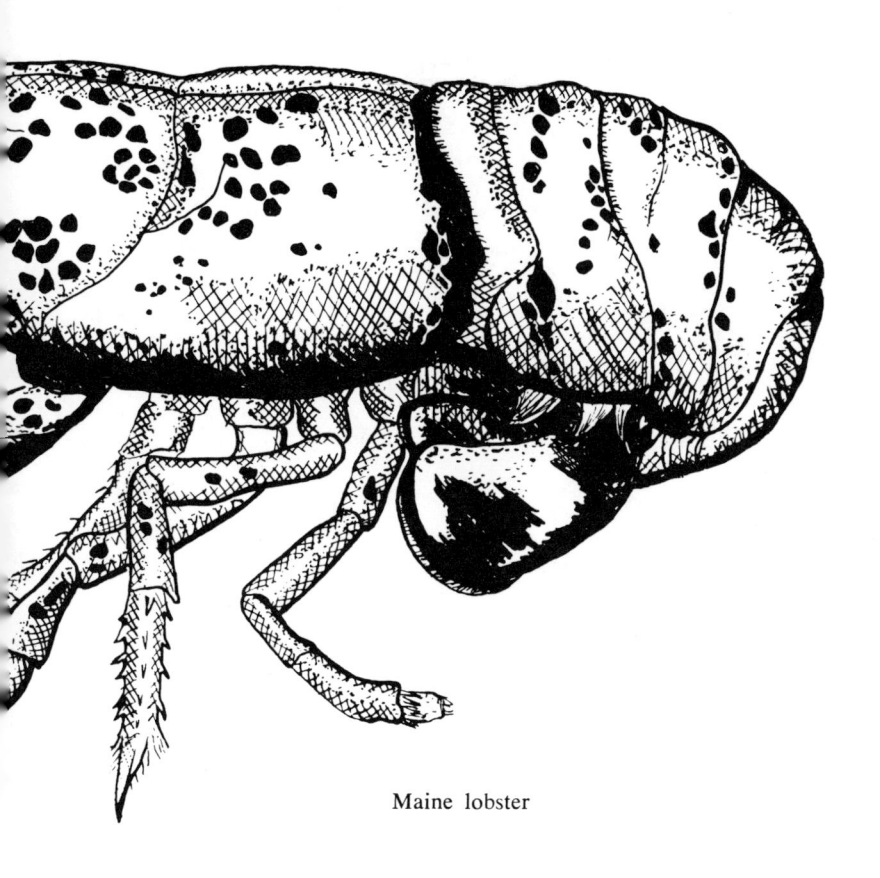

# LOBSTERS, RED AND GREEN

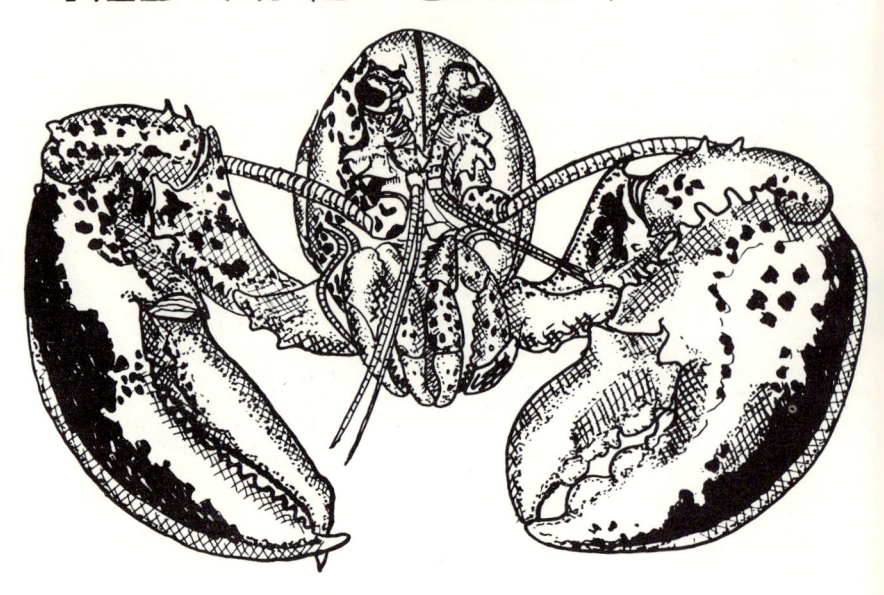

## CHAPTER 14

Almost any day you can see lobsters in the fish market. Sometimes they are red, meaning that they have been boiled, and sometimes they are a dark green-brown and still alive. It is easy to look at lobsters in a store, but just try to spy on them at the ocean, and you'll find it's a completely different story. They live just off the rocks conveniently near their food in water too deep for us to explore without diving equipment.

A lobster contents himself with a diet of mussels and clams. Mussels are easy to get. There are always numbers of them attached to the rocks and they are easily crushed and eaten. Clams are harder for a lobster to gather, and that is not because clams can run away or defend themselves. It is because a lobster must work for the clams he eats. He digs them out of the sand or mud on the ocean floor. Dished up on the crushed half-shell, clams suit the lobster perfectly. And they might suit many humans too, if they were served up a little more neatly. But if a lobster has had a bad day, and the supply of mussels and clams runs low, he will hungrily attack a fish or any other meaty, living creature that accidentally comes his way.

The food is pinched and crushed by one large claw, and cut up by the other, until it is a proper size for his dainty mouth with all its delicate, fast-moving parts. The mouth, for all the delicacy in handling the food, rips up and tears apart the pieces arriving from the claws and sends the shreds on inside to the stomach's grinding mill. Passage through the grinding mill mashes up all the fragments that have any shape at all, and now at last they are ready to nourish the hungry lobster.

The good juices removed from the food are pumped to every part of a lobster's body in blue-blooded blood vessels. The blood also carries oxygen so that the cells receiving nourishment from the food may turn it into energy and body tissue. A lobster is constantly moving, eating, and growing, so he must have a continuous supply of oxygen. He gets it from the sea water which is

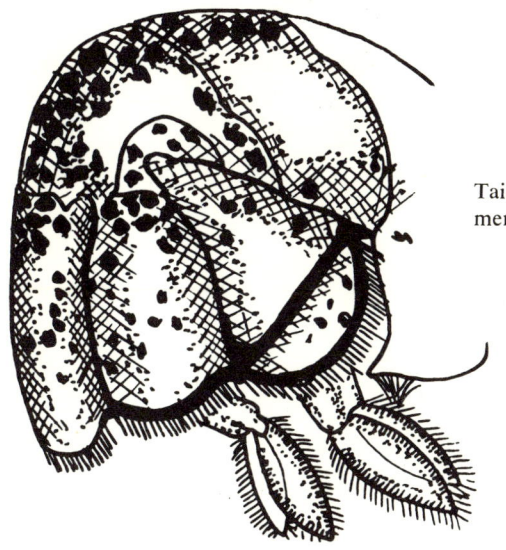

Tail, some joints of abdomen, and swimmerets

Diagram of lobster

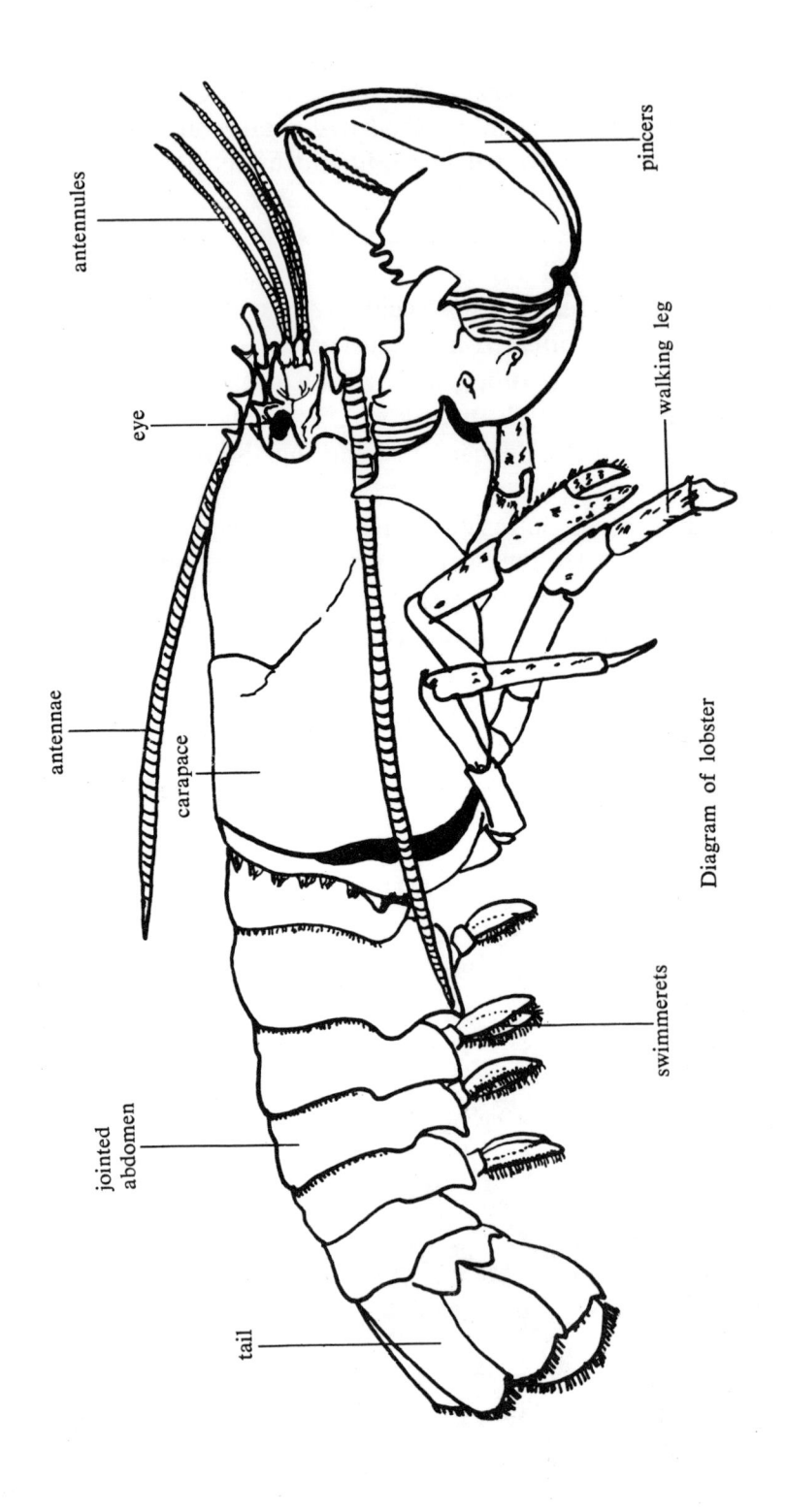

pumped in and out under the smooth hard shell on his back. The oxygen is taken from the water by gills that are attached underneath the carapace. The gills in turn pass it to the blood vessels.

The lobster's head and body are joined together under the carapace, and his abdomen, with its jointed covering, extends out behind. It is powerful and muscular, and although a lobster doesn't know it, it is delicious. With a flip of his abdomen under water a lobster can dart rapidly backward. Or he can boldly walk forward, gracefully holding up his claws in order not to trip on them. If you look closely as he bounces along on the sharp tips of four pairs of legs, you'll see his swimmerets going furiously, and begin to suspect he's not walking at all but that he's swimming. As he advances he waves his antennae around in the water, watching closely with his beady black eyes for enemies and for live food.

A lobster molts his shell in order to grow. This means that many times during his life he steps out of his old tight shell and replaces it. The new and larger one lies wrinkled and temporarily flexible on his soft body. It is

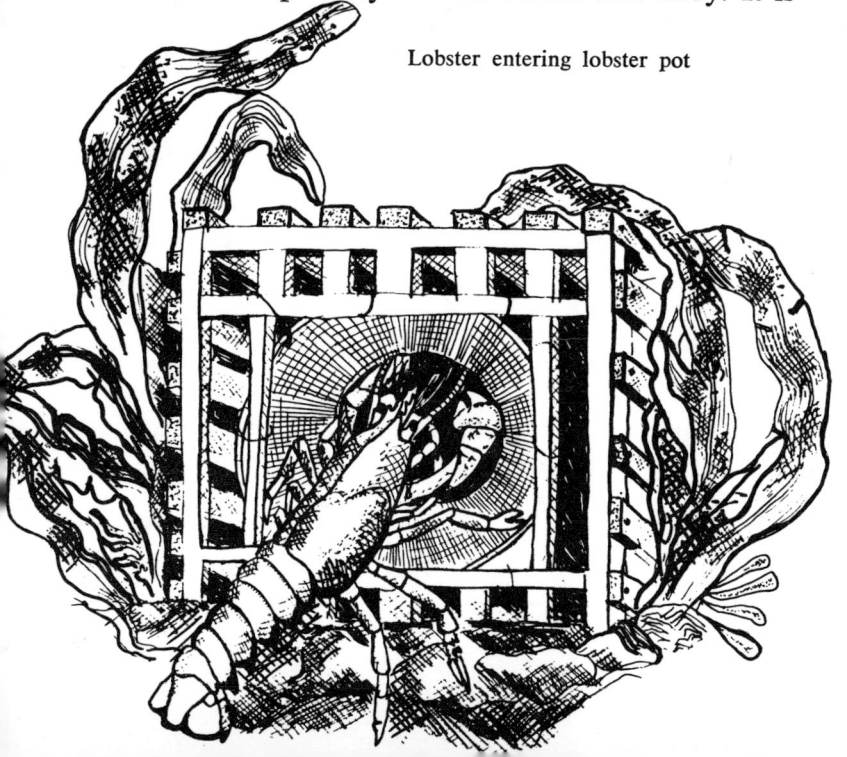

Lobster entering lobster pot

Ten thousand lobster eggs

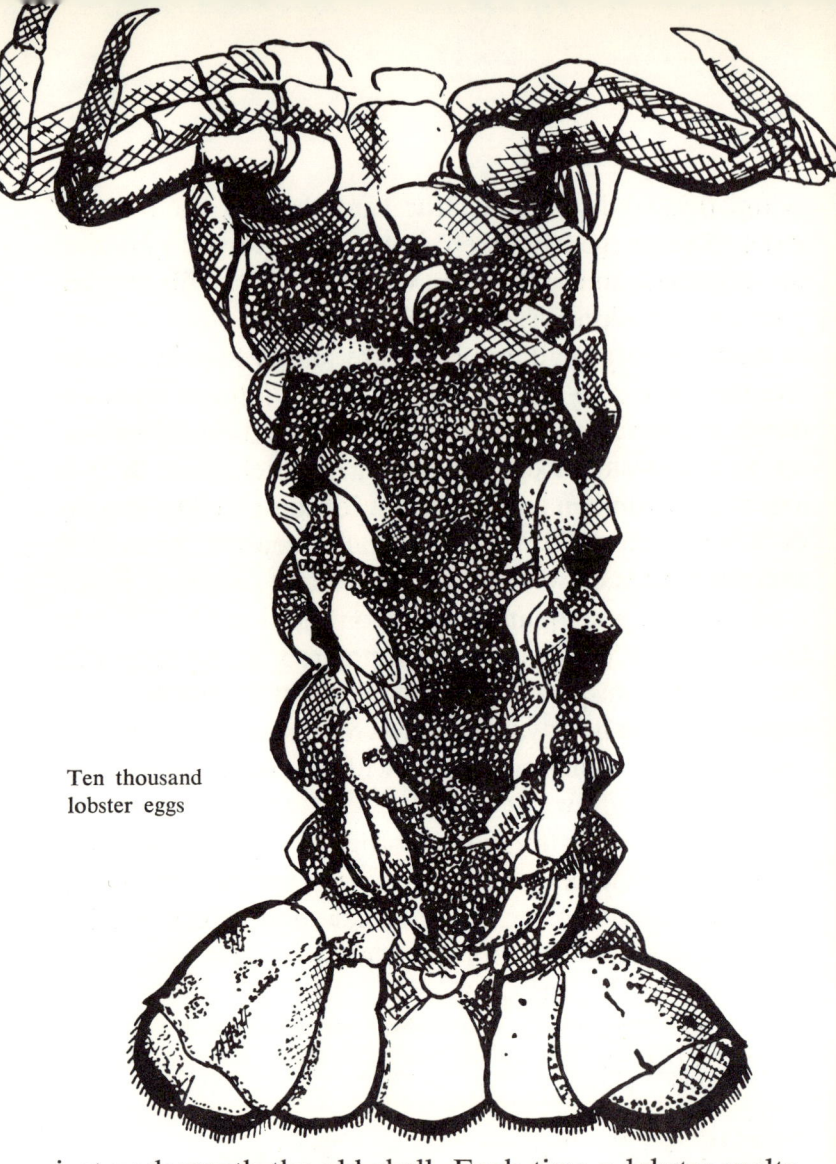

just underneath the old shell. Each time a lobster molts, he leaves behind the lining of his gullet, his stomach and intestine, the tough clear covering over each of his eyes, and the lining of his balancing sacs. When the old shell has split and with a good deal of effort the naked lobster emerges; he is vulnerable and must be very cautious. He would make a good meal without his tough armor to protect him. Even his claws are soft and useless. It is a time for him to hide.

But there is a job that cannot be overlooked. He has lost a grain of sand with the lining of each of his balancing organs, and must place a fresh grain in each one before his new shell hardens. Only with one grain of sand in a tiny hole at the base of each antenna can a lobster feel the force of gravity and tell which is up and which is down. A lobster once was tricked into thinking down was up, and up was down. Just after he molted, when he was looking for sand for the balancing sacs, he was placed on a bed of iron filings. So instead of sand he put a little iron filing in each hole. Everyone knows that iron filings and magnets get along famously. Iron filings crowd onto the metal of the magnet and stick there. So when a magnet was held over the head of the lobster with iron filings in his balancing sacs, the iron filings moved up to the top of the small spaces, drawn by magnetic energy. Immediately the lobster thought he must be upside down, for grains of sand would tickle the tops of the sacs only if he fell over in the water, and gravity pulled them there. So thinking he was upside down the lobster turned over. Then he was really helpless for his feet were waving in the water and his back was on the sand. All of his world was upside down, but his balancing sacs kept right on telling him that all was well. Luckily for the lobsters on the shore there is no one there to trick them into living on their backs.

All along the coast line, especially in Maine and Massachusetts, lobstermen sink their lobster pots. A lobster-pot buoy floats above each pot on the surface of the water. Every lobster fisherman has his own colors and special stripes, and he may work a whole series of pots. Each pot is baited and will let a lobster in but never let him out. The lobster's claws keep him stuck on the inside of the small circular entranceway. When the pots are hoisted out of the water the fisherman often finds some lobsters in his pots that are too small. A lobster less than 10½ inches has to be thrown back. That is because a lobster of this size has just begun to reproduce, and if it were not allowed to lay its eggs, the sea would soon shelter no more lobsters. A small lobster does not lay many eggs, the first season maybe around 10,000, but if it has a chance to grow and mature, it reproduces in enormous numbers. An old lobster may lay 100,000 eggs. In some places the old lobsters are protected by law.

The lobster eggs are fertilized by sperm received the year before and stored in pockets behind the female's legs. After the eggs are made fertile and start to develop, the mother lobster glues them to the swimmerets on her abdomen. They stay there, where they get lots of oxygen from the water, from early spring through the following winter until the warmer waters of the new spring. Finally they hatch into larvae, that go through several changes of form in the plankton, until they look like miniature lobsters. Five years later each lobster is ready for market, and that's where you are likely to see him.

VOCABULARY

buoy — *an anchored marker that floats on the top of the water*
grinding mill — *a three-section grinder for reducing food to tiny fragments*
gullet — *tube leading from the mouth to the stomach*
magnetic energy — *powerful attraction of a magnet for bits of iron*
swimmerets — *small flaps on the bottom of the abdomen that help the lobster to swim and hold eggs laid by the female*

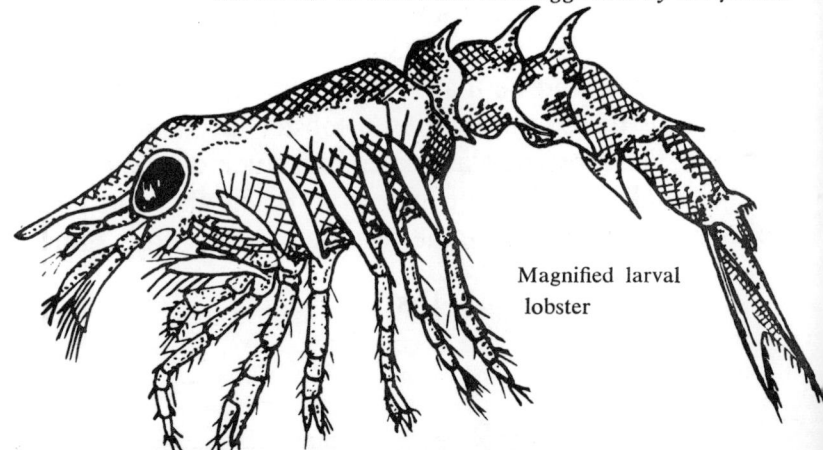

Magnified larval lobster